SOAR

BIBLE STUDY

Dig deeper to be lifted higher

Amy Groeschel
Sheri Yates

Publisher iKAN Publishing

SOAR

Copyright © 2014 by Amy Groeschel and Sheri Yates

This title is also available as a Kindle e-book.

This is a study guide that can be paired with our video-based Bible study at www.soarwithgod.com.

We would love to hear from you. Find us on Facebook at https://www.facebook.com/SOARwithgod

ISBN-10: 149611017X

ISBN-13: 978-1496110176

All Scripture quotations, unless otherwise indicated, are taken from the Holy Bible, New International Version 1984 (NIV). Other Scripture references are from the King James Version (KJV), New American Standard Bible (NASB), New Living Translation (NLT), and the New King James Version (NKJV). All emphasis added.

Cover and Interior design: iPublicidades

Editor: Adam M. Swiger

Printed in the United States of America

Dedication

SOAR is dedicated to every person that is seeking to know
God more intimately and deeply.
We pray that you will SOAR in your relationship
with HIM through Jesus Christ!

Contents

Find the video-based teaching for this Bible study at http://soarwithgod.com.

A note from the authors

To the beloved in Christ,

The SOAR study that you are about to begin was born out of a vision from God, a call to discipleship, and a LOVE for you. That's right. My love, Sheri's love, but infinitely greater, God's love for *you*! Sheri and I believe that these four eight-week studies will take you to a deeper level with God. Our prayer is that you'll be on fire and madly in love with your God.

This study is simple. It is going to get you into the Word of God. The Holy Spirit will be the ultimate teacher. If you give yourself to this journey, you will never be the same! We are honored to be a part of building you up to a fuller maturity in Christ Jesus.

> The Lord is the everlasting God, the Creator of the ends of the earth. He will not grow tired or weary, and his understanding no one can fathom. He gives strength to the weary and increases the power of the weak. Even youths grow tired and weary, and young men stumble and fall; but those who hope in the Lord will renew their strength. They will soar on wings like eagles; they will run and not grow weary, they will walk and not be faint. (Isaiah 40:28-31)

Loving you and Loving Him,

Amy Groeschel

Dear friends,

As an abused child, my desperate mission was to try to find my worth and value in anything—excelling in school, working hard at my job, friends, boys/men, parents, family, college, and my career. It was like there was a hole in the bottom of my heart! All things fell short. Nothing—no job—no person—no possession—no amount of money or vindication can bring peace into our lives!

God is in the redemption business. Today I am healed and restored in every way. I am free! I am alive! The redemption of Christ is also available to you. He wants you to be well, to prosper you, and not to harm you in anyway.

Amy and I pray for you to know Him and His will for you so intimately that you see His fingerprints all over your life, live by the Spirit in every way, and burn with passion for Him—that you SOAR with Him all the days of your life and, in return, change the world one life at a time!

> Now the Lord is the Spirit, and where the Spirit of the Lord is, there is freedom.
> (2 Corinthians 3:17)

Love in Christ,

Sheri Yates

Introduction
Welcome to SOAR!

When we know God intimately, we soar! To soar is to climb swiftly or powerfully. The power of God is available to you to overcome and live in freedom! SOAR (a four-part video based Bible study) is designed to create in you a longing to know our loving God more and more fully. To know Him is to know the love and the power of the living God, which can soar far above any mountain in your life. Spiritual growth begins and is maintained in intimate fellowship with the living God through Jesus Christ.

SOAR can be used individually, but for maximum blessings we hope that you can experience it in a group as well.

You will learn to seek God, obtain truth from reading and studying the Bible, strengthen your ability to walk in the Spirit more than your flesh, and diligently pursue the calling that God has for your life through Reach. You will never be the same.

When you **SOAR,** you:

God is orderly. Seeking Him should always come first. Seek God first for relationship, not for results.

Through seeking to know Him with all of your heart, you will find Him. His Word will become meaningful and personal to you. As you trust Him and His Word takes root in your heart, you will learn to walk by His voice. You will learn to discern God's voice. Once you have learned to hear and obey God, He can direct your daily steps, which enables you to fulfill His purposes on this earth!

It's a continuing process of seeking God, renewing your mind, keeping in step with the Spirit, and reaching out to others.

Let's look at the key scriptures that fuel the vision for what we will explore in our study time together.

SEEK GOD

Know God Intimately.

> "But seek first his kingdom and his righteousness, and all these things will be given to you as well." (Matthew 6:33)

OBTAIN TRUTH

Find Freedom in God's Word.

> "Then you will know the truth, and the truth will set you free." (John 8:32)

ABIDE

Live by the Spirit of God.

> "Since we live by the Spirit, let us keep in step with the Spirit." (Galatians 5:25)

REACH OUT

Share the Good News.

> "The harvest is plentiful, but the workers are few. Ask the Lord of the harvest, therefore, to send out workers into his field." (Matthew 9:37)

Leader Guide for SOAR

LEAD!   Pray, Prepare, Lead, Love, Seek
SHARE!   Small-Group Time
EAT!   Study Time
SERVE!   Give Back
LIVE!   Fellowship
LEAD!   Leader Preparation

Leaders, you were called for a time such as this! We want you to love leading your group, building meaningful relationships with them and becoming an even more sold-out follower of Christ!

PRAY for yourself and your group members.

PREPARE by seeking God daily and being in the Word. Be prepared to get the group discussion started by sharing your own personal-growth moments.

LEAD by example. Don't allow any one person to dominate the discussion (this includes you). Teach them how to study the Bible. Lead their hearts away from distractions to the greatness of God's love and presence. Lead them to seek God for relationship rather than results.

LOOK for wounds, bondage, and practical needs in those you lead. Create a safe environment. A good leader cares and is sensitive to the needs of God's people because he loves them. Pray and ask God for discernment.

LOVE your group with prayer. Pour into them. Know what is going on in their lives. Help them find a mentor or whatever they need. Write them a note to build them up and encourage them in the Lord! You are a light upon a hill. Love them as Jesus would.

SEEK. Search the people in your group to find their special gifts, callings, and talents. Encourage them to fully utilize the gifts you see in them.

SHARE! Small-group time

Our heart's goals for small-group time are:

- that each person will have a safe environment so that he or she can be transparent.
- that members will develop meaningful connections to begin building true, biblical community with one another.

Here are some suggested ideas for your small-group time:

- Discuss the previous week's study lessons.
- Pray and worship together.
- Teach your own short lesson (10-15 min.) to the group.
- Have a sign-up for members of the group to give a devotion (mini-lesson) or testimony. Sometimes you need to ask them personally to do this. Encourage them past their fears or apathy.

Again, we encourage you to be transparent with your own personal examples so that your group will follow your lead.

EAT! Nourishment—Individual study time

This is your daily bread (otherwise known as quiet time). Consider this as being as vital to your well being as the food you eat. Jesus said, "I am the bread of life. He who comes to me will never go hungry..." (John 6:35). Each week of the study, you will obtain truth for yourself. Hold your group accountable in completing their weekly assignments. Ask your group members what would help them to complete their study. They should write down their answers, as should you, to help remind them to implement their strategy. However, keep in mind that growing in their relationship with God is more important than completing the homework assignment.

CRAVE! More study time

There is a Crave section at the bottom of most days. This section is designed for the person who just didn't get enough from the homework and wants more scriptures or more truth.

SERVE! Loving others

Be intentional servers! Identify serving opportunities within the group, in the community, or within your church. If someone you know needs prayer, take your group to pray with him or her. If someone has a family member at a nursing home, take your group there. Maybe you could even go on a mission trip together! Check with your church mission's leader for more ideas to engage in serving others. Consider assigning a group member a leadership role for planning and communicating your ministry ideas.

LIVE! Fellowship

Share life together. Spend time together just talking about the Lord and all the good things He has done. Develop prayer partners, mentors, and accountability friends. Throw parties and have dinner together. Share in Communion. Help each other out with life's emergencies and share the moments for celebration. Cry and rejoice together. Enjoy each other!

PART 1

SEEK GOD

"But seek first his kingdom and his righteousness,
and all these things will be given to you as well."

(Matthew 6:33)

SEEK GOD:
Study Outline

Week 1: Seek to know and love God. Turn your burdens and wounds over to God and seek Him.

Week 2: Seek to know God's character through the Word.

Week 3: Seek to know God's names and character.

Week 4: Seek to know God the Creator.

Week 5: Seek to know God through prayer.

Week 6: Seek to know God through prayer that rests, listens and delights in His presence.

Week 7: Seek to know God through intercessory prayer, petitions, and faith.

Week 8: Seek to know God through worship.

> "Love the Lord your God with all your heart and with all your soul and with all your mind and with all your strength." (Mark 12:30)

Find the videos under the SEEK GOD tab at www.soarwithgod.com.

SEEK GOD – Week One
Know and Love God
SHARE!

Objective: To turn your burdens over to God and to seek, to know, and love Him with all your heart

Memory Verse:

> Come to Me, all you who are weary and burdened, and I will give you rest. Take my yoke upon you and learn from me, for I am gentle and humble in heart, and you will find rest for your souls. For my yoke is easy and my burden is light. (Matthew 11:28-30)

God longs for you to know Him personally.

When you were born, someone cared for you. You slept, ate, cried, and pooped (yes, you did—everyone poops!). You couldn't do *anything*. You could only rest and be nurtured. As you spent time with your family, you connected with them and built a relationship.

Some of us had wonderful relationships and others had painful ones. My (Sheri's) family life had some difficult challenges. However, there is good news for those of us who had painful family experiences: when you receive Jesus Christ as your Savior, you are adopted into His family! You are now born of God. Read John 1:13. This verse means so much to me because it clarifies that I am in God's family and that adoption cannot be annulled!

It is time to get to know God the Father just as you got to know your family. God is your lifeline in this new life with Jesus. You need to rest in Him and allow Him to take your burdens. Spend time with Him today!

God has pursued a relationship with mankind since the creation of the world. First, He created us, breathed His own life into us, walked with us, dwelt among us after the fall of man, and then made a way for us to know Him personally again by sending His Son to shed His blood as the final sacrifice for us. Yet most of us only know *about* God. We don't really know Him in a personal and intimate way.

There is a difference between knowing about someone and knowing someone personally. Most of us know about the President of our country, but we don't know him personally. On the other hand, if you are married, hopefully you know your spouse intimately.

What can you do to know God like this? *prayer, read the bible, talk to him*

You must seek God with all of your heart.

There can be many hindrances that keep us from intimacy.

Someone might have wounded you, or perhaps something has caused your heart to be closed or hesitant toward God. Maybe you believe that you are not good enough for Him. Maybe you've been deceived and have turned your heart to something or someone other than God. Whatever it is, you can overcome it through Christ Jesus. When our hearts are wounded, angry, bitter, or closed to people, then our hearts are most likely closed to God also.

Have you ever built a wall to shut off your heart to someone? I certainly have! The truth is, holding onto our wounds and pain really only hurts us. We need to bring the pain and wounds out of hiding and into the Light so that we can begin to open our hearts back up to God.

To seek God with all of your heart, you have to:

- Be willing to open your heart to Him.
- Ask God for His help!

GROUP SHARE TIME

Break into groups of two.

Read one or more of these passages to each other:
Luke 11:45-46; Psalm 139:1-7; Matthew 11:28-30.

- What heavy load are you carrying around? *Career, family, isolation*
- What is distracting you from seeking God? *work, frustrations, emotions, insecurities*

Write down those things and seal them in an envelope addressed to God. Commit to the group that you will not pick them back up. Hang the envelope at home somewhere to remind you that your life is now hidden in Christ Jesus.

Gather back as a group:

- Share your responses.
- Pray for and minister to one another.

You will need to have a SOAR notebook.

SEEK GOD – Week One
Know and Love God
EAT!

Objective: To turn your burdens over to God and to seek, to know, and love Him with all your heart

Memory Verse:

> Come to me, all you who are weary and burdened, and I will give you rest. Take my yoke upon you and learn from me, for I am gentle and humble in heart, and you will find rest for your souls. For my yoke is easy and my burden is light. (Matthew 11:28-30)

The eagle is such a beautiful creature! Did you know that its body is approximately four feet long; its wingspan is eight feet wide; but it only weighs about eight pounds? It's no wonder that the eagle *SOAR*s with such grace and magnificence. It is hardly carrying any weight at all!

I (Sheri) want to SOAR with God like that eagle! Soaring with God allows us to see everything from a new perspective. My daughter was seven years old when she took her first airplane ride. She said, "Mommy, from up here, all those things that look so big seem so small. You can't even see them from up here."

It's all about perspective. Soaring with God gives us life that is truly *life*!

It's time to lay down the past. Lay down all those things that burden you and all of the distractions that keep you from seeking God. Throw off everything that keeps you from soaring with God!

- Begin each day turning your mind and heart to God.
- Enter into your time in the Word with a hunger and thirst for His presence.
- Ask the Holy Spirit to guide you into all truth (read John 16:13).

Do not rush the lessons or feel the need to complete a task. This is your time to spend with "Daddy." Enjoy, delight in, and savor the Word.

> In the beginning was the Word, and the Word was with God, and the Word was God. (John 1:1)

Day 1   Goals

Read Deuteronomy 6:4-9 and Matthew 22:34-40.

Grab your SOAR notebook. We are going to evaluate where we are today—whether good, bad, ugly, or great. Be real with your answers. Set a goal for where you want to be in one year. Remember, "where there is no vision [no redemptive revelation of God], the people perish" (Proverbs 29:18a AMP). Underline where you are today. Circle where you would like to be in one year.

1. Based on the way you live your life today (i.e., spend your time and money), how well would you say that you are keeping the first and greatest commandment—to love God with all your heart, mind, soul, and strength?

    - Never
    - Sometimes
    - Many times
    - Consistently
    - Always

2. On an average day, how is your relationship with God? Underline where you are today. Circle where you would like to be in one year.

    Are you *cold, lukewarm,* or *hot*? Take a look at Revelation 3:15-16.

    Where are you?
    - Losing momentum
    - Flat
    - Growing slowly
    - Growing quickly
    - Soaring

What are you doing in your walk that caused you to answer Question #2 the way you did?

- Not seeking
- Seeking minimally
- Seeking consistently
- Clinging to Him for most
- Clinging to Him for everything

Spend time today praying and thinking about your answers.

Day 2   You are Known

Read Psalm 139 and Romans 8:38-39.

God knows you! God loves you! He longs to be loved and known by you. In your SOAR notebook, write out your favorite verse(s) today and even record some thoughts to God in response to His love for you. Enjoy Him all day long!

Day 3   Bye-Bye Anixiousness

Read Psalm 143.

This psalm was like a daily medication for me (Amy) around nine years ago. I was consumed with worry over my health. I became anxious about the possibility of an early death. After several months of feeling defeated, God convicted me of my lack of faith and trust in Him. I began to recite and meditate on Psalm 143:8. I overcame my fear with the truth that nothing could separate me from God's love ... *not even death*! I am free!

Is your heart heavy? Are you worried and anxious with *what ifs*? Memorize a favorite verse from this psalm today. Write it out. Read it aloud (repeat these steps until you know it) and meditate on it continually today.

> Do not be anxious about anything, but in everything, by prayer and petition, with thanksgiving, present your requests to God. And the peace of God, which transcends all understanding, will guard your hearts and your minds in Christ Jesus. (Philippians 4:6-7)

In case you were wondering what "anything" and "everything" meant, we looked it up for you. "Anything" means *anything*! "Everything" means *everything*!

What are you anxious about? Write it down in your SOAR notebook, pray about it, and give it to God. Continue to pray about it, but don't be anxious about it. Only worry about it when you conclude that God is not taking care of it.

Day 4   Seek First

Read Matthew 6: 19-34 and Philippians 3:4-14.

> "But seek first his kingdom and his righteousness, and all these things will be given to you as well." (Matthew 6:33)

What does seeking God look like in your life? *prayer, diving in the word*

Feelings of guilt used to sometimes drive my desire to spend time with God in prayer and Scripture reading. I guess I thought that I was letting God down. Honestly, I assume God must feel disappointed when we neglect Him. After all, He tells us in the Word that He is a jealous God. I'm jealous for time with the people I love, too. Here's the deal: God doesn't want us to come to Him out of obligation. When you and I see God for who He really is, we desire Him, period. Oh, Father, open our eyes to who you are!

Write, pray, or meditate on this today. Tell God that you want to know Him and love Him more. Cry out to Him for more of His presence in your life.

Ask God for more effective faith in Him and His Word.

> And without faith it is impossible to please God, because anyone who comes to him must believe that he exists and that he rewards those who earnestly seek him. (Hebrews 11:6)

The word earnest means serious and sincere.

Day 5   Cling

Read this slowly! Make it your prayer and heart's desire.

> O God, you are my God, earnestly I seek you; my soul thirsts for you, my body longs for you, in a dry and weary land where there is no water. I have seen you in the sanctuary and beheld your power and your glory. Because your love is better than life, my lips will glorify you. I will praise you as long as I live, and in your name I will lift up my hands. My soul will be satisfied as with the richest of foods; with singing lips my mouth will praise you. On my bed I remember you; I think of you through the watches of the night. Because you are my help, I sing in the shadow of your wings. My soul clings to you; your right hand upholds me. (Psalm 63:1-8)

CRAVE

Read Isaiah 40 and soar with God!

Read Psalm 42 and seek God's help in your trials.

SEEK GOD – Week Two
Know God's Character
SHARE!

Week One Review Question: What burden did you lay down in order to seek God more? *family and career*

Objective: Seeking to know God's character through the Word

Memory Verse:

> "For where your treasure is, there your heart will be also." (Matthew 6:21)

Have you ever won a grand prize, door prize, or anything? One year at the state fair, when I (Sheri) was a child, I won three large prizes. I played games the rest of the evening for free because everyone who saw my prizes asked me to try to win them a prize, too. It was fun! I didn't even consider giving one of them away or sharing them with my little sister. They were my treasure. Like Matthew 6:21 says, my heart was there also.

Consider what you have treasured in your life—maybe a wedding ring, a new car, your first home, a child, a spouse, your work, or maybe you even won the lottery. All of those treasures pale in comparison to the love of God through Jesus Christ. He is the greatest treasure!

Get real and be honest. Right now, what is your greatest treasure? *family* What are you seeking? *family* What do your heart and mind continually turn toward? The answer probably lies in how you spend your time and money. Look at the way Jesus said it in our memory verse:

> "Seek the Kingdom of God above all else, and live righteously, and he will give you everything you need." (Matthew 6:33)

Our goal, our aim, and our yearning desire should be to know Christ!

So why don't we pursue and desire God more? Like me, maybe you have roadblocks that keep you from seeking God.

What are some roadblocks?

Roadblock 1 – Too busy: "I want to have time for God, but I just don't have time!" If we really want to do something, we will create a way. If this is you, then God is not first. Ouch! We must *plan* time to seek God.

> "If you fail to plan, you are planning to fail." ~ Benjamin Franklin

I am a busy mom of three children, whom I home school. Sometimes I get so busy that I when I do stop, I realize that I have not even acknowledged God's presence with me. Whether we realize it or not, God is present all the time because he lives in us through the Holy Spirit. How do I get over this roadblock? I just acknowledge God like a member of our family. We talk about or talk to God all day long—throughout our schoolwork, eating, watching a movie, or interacting with other people. We just include Him in everything instead of making Him an additional thing that we do.

Roadblock 2 – Disobedience: Christ recreated us as holy, but disobedience and sin cause our hearts to harden toward God. Our hard-heartedness is a roadblock to experiencing the fullness of Him. Fully surrendering our lives to Him sets us free.

Roadblock 3 – Apathetic: Maybe you suppose, "I've tried quiet time with God, and it wasn't so great." So you gave up. That was my life for a long time. I would pray for a minute and be bored. I didn't feel anything nor get anything out of my time. I was lukewarm. How I got past this was through reading the Bible. As I read the Bible and learned who God is, I longed to know Him more, pray more, and spend more time with Him.

How can you and I eliminate these roadblocks?

- **Tell God about it.** Tell Him you want to desire and love Him more. Continue praying until your heart changes. Seek Him and you will find Him. Celebrate the small ways you see God break down roadblocks!

- **Make God your daily nourishment.** Jesus is the Bread of Life. He is the Living Water. Does your body require daily food and water? Sure it does! Your spirit is no different. Nourish it daily. And if you're wondering how to nourish your spirit, start simple: pray, read the bible, and turn your thoughts to God.

GROUP SHARE TIME

Your treasure map to knowing God better is right in front of you: It is the Bible. Let's open it!

Break into small groups. Read the memory verse (Matthew 6:21) aloud.

- If a newspaper reporter observed you all day today, what would they list on the front page of the paper as your *greatest treasure*, based on the way you spent your day? _work_
- What steps can you take tomorrow so that Jesus Christ is your greatest treasure? _bring god into it_
- Name your roadblocks. _too busy, distracted, emotions_
- Is God scheduled daily into your life? Is there a planned time to meet with God, or do you fit Him in when it's convenient? If you have a scheduled time, are you keeping it? If not, schedule God on your calendar. Tell each other about your scheduled time; commit to it; and hold each other accountable.
- Be real and transparent with each other. Confess your lapses in seeking Him to one another and pray for and encourage each other.
- Celebrate each other's successes as your daily walk with God transforms and improves.
- Gather back as a group to share what you found.

Go on a Treasure Hunt!

Read one of the following passages and list below the character traits of God that you find: Psalm 83; Matthew 5; John 17; Psalm 99; Psalm 103; Ephesians 1.

SEEK GOD – Week Two
Know God's Character
EAT!

Objective: Seeking to know God's character through the Word

Memory Verse:

"For where your treasure is, there your heart will be also." (Matthew 6:21)

SEEK GOD

Begin each day by turning your mind, heart, and eyes to God. Enter into your time in the Word with a hunger and thirst for His presence. "Ask the Holy Spirit to guide you into all truth" (John 16:13).

Do not rush the lessons or feel the need to complete them as a task on your to-do list. This is your time to spend with "Father." Enjoy, delight in, and savor the Word. "In the beginning was the Word, and the Word was with God, and the Word was God" (John 1:1).

Day 1   Be Still

Establish a regular quiet time (even if it's five minutes).

Today ask God to give you a hunger and thirst for Him. Read Psalm 23 and take time to relish in your Shepherd!

It is God's will that you seek Him. To know God, our hearts must intentionally look for Him. I (Amy) grew up attending church. I received my salvation at an early age. Little did I know, as a child, that God's Word was active and alive and that the Word has divine power to change me into the image of my Creator. I studied much of God's Word, and it caused me to grow as a Christian. It taught me who God is. The sad thing, though, is that I neglected my relationship with God. In my youth, I ignored much of His Word. I got caught up in finding my identity through my peers (many of whom were unbelievers), which corrupted my character. I have grievous regret over my wasted years. Yet I praise God for His faithfulness and patience with me!

It is very painful to feel neglected, isn't it? It feels a bit like rejection. God desires a relationship with you! Throw off every distraction and desire the One—for He alone can satisfy.

Day 2   Know God More

Create a list of "Character Traits of God" in your SOAR notebook.

Read Exodus 33 and 34 and record His character traits (e.g., loving, merciful, etc.). You might need to finish this assignment tomorrow. If so, that's just fine! Your focus should be on enjoying God and His Word. *Traits of God: Merciful, Father, Love, forgiving, Gracious, Friend, companion, healer, promise, light life giving, just*

Day 3   Reflect

Finish Day 2, then read through your character traits list.

Take some time to quietly reflect on who God is. Read 2 Corinthians 3:7-18. Spending time in God's presence changes us. What is changing in you? Tell God about it. Maybe tell someone else, too. Try writing about it. *everything*

Day 4   Attitude Assessment

Read Philippians 2:1-15.

Add to the character traits list.

Respond to the following questions:

- What does your attitude usually look like? *Depends on the days events and place*
- Does it resemble the attitude of Christ? *sometimes*

Spend time meditating on the nature of Jesus. Ask the Father to change you more and more into the image of His Son.

Day 5   I Love You Lord

Read this slowly. Make it your prayer and heart's desire:

> I love you, O LORD, my strength. The LORD is my rock, my fortress and my deliverer; my God is my rock, in whom I take refuge. He is my shield and the horn of my salvation, my stronghold. I call to the LORD, who is worthy of praise, and I am saved from my enemies. (Psalm 18:1-3)

Consider memorizing this text.

CRAVE

- Read the book of Colossians. It is not long, but it is, oh, so rich!
- Read Psalm 18—the whole chapter.

SEEK GOD – Week Three
Know God's Names and Character
SHARE!

Week Two Review Question: Name one of God's character traits that meant the most to you this past week. Explain. Restorer: he is the healer and restorer of all

Objective: Seeking to know God's names and character

Memory Verse:

> "Now this is eternal life: that they may know you, the only true God, and Jesus Christ, whom you have sent." (John 17:3)

It's easy to know about people, but it is harder to know them personally. For example, if I saw Craig, Senior Pastor of Lifechurch.tv, and ran up to say "hi," he might look at me with that "and you must be…?" look. Then it would dawn on me that I know him but he doesn't know me. There is a difference in knowing about someone and really knowing—having a relationship with—him or her.

> Not everyone who says to me, "Lord, Lord," will enter the kingdom of heaven, but only he who does the will of my Father who is in heaven. Many will say to me on that day, "Lord, Lord, did we not prophesy in your name, and in your name drive out demons and perform many miracles?" Then I will tell them plainly, "I never knew you. Away from me, you evildoers!" (Matthew 7:21-23)

Clearly, knowing God is what life is all about!

Let's examine how we can seek to know God more intimately.

Names and nicknames tell a little bit about who we are or how others may see us. I (Sheri) had many nicknames when I was growing up, like "short stuff" (because I was short, though powerful) and "motor mouth" (because I never stopped talking).

Fellowship and Ice Breaker: Have everyone share how they got their names and nicknames.

Do you know that God has many names? They tell us more about who He is. Some are endearing, like a sweet expression of love (Comforter or Father). As we get to know God by seeking His names and character traits throughout the Word, we will enter into a fuller, more intimate relationship with Him.

How we know God? To keep it simple, I like to relate this to how I get to know a new friend. In your group, prepare a list or just discuss how you would get to know a new friend.

If we seek to know God in the Word—as we would complete a word- search game—we will find God's names, which define his character. Let's dig in!

Spend time with them... Find out what makes them

GROUP SHARE TIME *happy, sad, excited, hurt. What are their comfort*

Look up John 10. Compile a list of character traits revealed in these verses. Celebrate God's wonderful names and character!

Shepherd   Jesus   Father   Str
gate keeper   messiah   son

Names and Character of God	Verse
Authority	
Calls you by name	3
Full Life	10
Gate	7
Goes ahead of you	4
Good Shepherd	2
He speaks—His voice can be heard	3
Lays down his life	11
Leads you	3
Obeys the Father's commands—sinless	18
Provider—finds pasture; food; provision	9
Savior	9
Takes up His life—resurrection	17
Unity—one flock and one Shepherd	16

SEEK GOD – Week Three
Know God's Names and Character
EAT!

Objective: To search through the Bible to find the names and character of God so that we can know Him more intimately.

Memory Verse:

> "Now this is eternal life: that they may know you, the only true God, and Jesus Christ, whom you have sent." (John 17:3)

Seeking God on our own is a wonderful opportunity to know God. Seeking Him to know Him through the Word is a privilege. About 500 years ago, we didn't even have access to the written Word. People died so that we could have a Bible today! May we never take this for granted.

These suggested assignments are to help you to grow and seek God. They are not required, nor should you feel guilty if you don't complete them. If you have five minutes to spend, spend five. If you have thirty minutes, spend thirty. Ask God to lead you and give you wisdom and insight.

It's Word Search Week! I (Sheri) love word searches. I used to do them often as a child. When I really started reading the Bible, I noticed words everywhere that described God and His character. I began circling them in my Bible. I love to pick up my Bible today and see just how awesome God is when I see all of those circled words!

Pick one or more of the following Scripture passages to read every day this week. As you read the passages, look for the names of God. Use the Names of God chart (following this section) as a tool to help you find them. You may want to underline or circle God's character traits in your Bible or keep a growing list in your SOAR notebook.

Suggested Daily Readings:

Matthew 26:36-56; John 15:1-17; Ephesians 1; *Day 3*

Matthew 11:25-29; John 14; John 8:1-11; Jeremiah 1; *Day 2*

Luke 15; John 13:1-17; Isaiah 11:1-5; Habakkuk 3:17-19; *Day 1*

Colossians 1:15-20; John 11:1-44

[handwritten at top:] truth, justice, fair, righteous lord, wisdom, understanding counsel, might, knowledge

Day 1   Yielded

Select and read a passage from above. *[handwritten arrow pointing up]*

What character traits of God did you find? Did you already know this about God? *[handwritten: yes]* If not, renew your mind by writing them out, reading them aloud, or meditating on them throughout the day.

One of my favorites from John 15 is that Father God is the Gardener. I love this verse because it is a picture of a Gardener and a garden. The Gardener does all of the work; the plants in the garden just have to *receive*. This teaches me that I just need to learn to be a good receiver. I would write in my notebook: "God is the Gardener—He gives me all the nourishment I need. I just have to receive it by yielding my heart to Him!"

Day 2   Chosen

[handwritten: Salvation, Sovereign,]

Select and read a passage from above. *[handwritten arrow pointing up]*

What names or character traits did you find in your reading today? I will share one of my favorites, from Jeremiah 1, with you: God is relational. He chose me. He is so merciful that He chose me personally—how encouraging! I would write in my notebook: "God is intimate. He chose me." Now write your thoughts and prayers.

Day 3   Favorite Word

[handwritten: Isaiah 11: 1-5]

Select and read a passage from above. *[handwritten arrow pointing up]*

From the readings this week, what has been your favorite passage? Commit it to memory today.

Day 4   Character Review

Select and read a passage from above. *[handwritten: Provider]*

What name or character trait of God is especially in your mind this week? Thank God for it in prayer today.

Day 5   Rest

Schedule time to rest; be still (even if for just five minutes) and listen. Meditate on the names and character traits of God on the following page. Add to the list. When finances are short, thank God that He is the Provider. When a loved one is lost, thank God that He is our Comfort and that He hears our prayers. Who is God to you right now? Circle your answers on the chart.

[handwritten:] Comfort
peace
provider
pursuer

CRAVE

Pick any chapter of the Bible. Search for and underline God's names and character traits in your Bible. This is one of my favorite things to do. It reminds me of how awesome He is!

Week Three –
NAMES AND CHARACTER OF GOD

MOST HIGH GOD	DELIVERER	FORTRESS
CREATOR	I AM!	ABBA FATHER
THE LORD MY BANNER	ALL-KNOWING	ABUNDANT
PROVIDER	ABOVE ALL	BEGINNING
RESTORER	BRIDEGROOM	BREAD OF LIFE
THE LORD OF LORDS	JUST	IMMANUEL
KING OF KINGS	JESUS!	LAMB OF GOD
EVERLASTING GOD	LOVE	LIVING WATER
SHEPHERD	COMFORTER	PROTECTED
HEALER	DWELLING PLACE	FRIEND
MASTER	REDEEMER	TEACHER
ALL-SUFFICIENT ONE	SHEPHERD	WAY
SAVIOR	PROTECTOR	OMNISCIENT
TRUTH	NAME ABOVE ALL NAMES	NEAR
EQUIPPER	HOLY	GOOD
PRINCE OF PEACE	RIGHTEOUS	MERCIFUL
FAITHFUL	UNCHANGING	OMNIPOTENT
OMNIPRESENT	SOVEREIGN	PURSUER

Challenge: Can you list more names or character traits of God from the reading this week?

Peace
Father

SEEK GOD – Week Four
Know God the Creator
SHARE!

Week Three Review Question: How did God reveal Himself to you last week?

Objective: Seeking to know God the Creator

Memory Verses:

> The heavens declare the glory of God; the skies proclaim the work of his hands. (Psalm 19:1)

> In the beginning God created the heavens and the earth. (Genesis 1:1)

God created the world and all of its contents. He created *you*. God created all the resources for everything our eyes can see today. Have you taken a fresh look around to see God's handiwork?

GROUP SHARE TIME

This week we are going to stop and smell the roses. We all need to slow down our pace and appreciate the gift of life and the world that our loving Creator gave us to enjoy.

We pray that the following passages will encourage you to see God in all of creation—every seed, every season, every weed, every leaf, and every person. God has made everything beautiful in its time.

Read the memory verse (above) and Ecclesiastes 3:11-14.

Keep these passages in mind for the following activities as we search to see God in a new way today.

"God Made That" Game

Look around the room for two minutes and have each individual create a list of all the objects in view that were created by God. *everything: literally*

Share your answers. If more than one person has the same answer, everyone crosses that answer off of his or her list. If the answer is unique, circle it. Score all circled items at the end. Consider a prize at the end of the game for the most unique answers.

Group Questions

- What is your favorite animal? dolphin

- In all of creation, what fascinates you the most? love

- Where else would you live just for the beauty (aesthetics)? Ireland, Okhahoma Paris

- Which do you love more?

    ○ Mountains or oceans? Why?
    ○ Sunrise or sunset? Why?
    ○ Warm or cool weather? Why?

If time permits try:

- watching Louie Gigllio's YouTube video about Laminin.
- watching a nature program.

SEEK GOD – Week Four
Know God the Creator
EAT!

Objective: To seek to know God the Creator

Memory Verse:

> The heavens declare the glory of God; the skies proclaim the work of his hands. (Psalm 19:1)

Our time with the Lord this week will be a real adventure if you take on the assignments with your whole heart. We desire a fresh look at our Creator. God wants to reveal His glory to you. Look around. You're going to see glimpses of His majesty!

Suggested Daily Scripture Readings:

Genesis 1 and 2; Psalm 8; Psalm 19; Psalm 104; Romans 1:18-32 with Romans 8:18-25; Romans 9:1-8; Isaiah 44-45

Begin each day asking God to reveal Himself through His Word.

Read a suggested Bible passage slowly and breathe in every detail, even though you may have read it numerous times before. You may want to stop from time to time and reflect on the significance of what you're reading. As you go along, realize and enjoy the presence of God with you and within you!

Try not to worry about or get hung up on parts of the Bible that you don't fully understand. By faith, the Holy Spirit, and persistence in studying the entire Word, you will grow more and more. "All Scripture is God-breathed and is useful for teaching, rebuking, correcting, and training in righteousness, so that the man of God may be thoroughly equipped for every good work" (2 Timothy 3:16).

After selecting and reading your Bible verses, choose an activity from the following suggestions or create your own.

1. Write down some thoughts in your SOAR notebook. Express these thoughts to God in a prayer of praise.

2. Friends and/or family might want to join you for the following:

- Watch the weather and choose the best day to take a walk outside. A nearby park might provide the right atmosphere. Let the Creator capture you!
- Watch a nature show on television or video. Your local library or the Internet will have some good selections, too.
- All that I (Amy) wanted for my last birthday was the Planet Earth videos, because to me, they preach the greatest sermon ever told (sorry, Craig)!
- Stargazing is brilliant for an awe-inspiring time. If it's cold, gather blankets and bring hot cocoa! Consider including your family or friends.
- Read a Scripture passage aloud. Write a favorite verse or two and place these in a prominent place in your home or car.
- If you like to dabble in arts and crafts, then create your own nature scene.
- If you encounter a day with good, puffy clouds, then go outside and lie down to watch them. Just don't look directly at the sun!
- Express your love to God in the way that best suits your personality. Sing, shout, dance, play an instrument, write poetry, or sit in quiet stillness and acknowledge His presence.

Here's an exercise to get your mind processing: Describe the character traits of God without using any of your previous knowledge of Him through the Word of God or His people. Try to understand Him from what has been made by Him (not through circumstances that have been brought about through sin or the curse of sin). An example would be that God must be creative because of the pallet of colors that He has provided. Keep a growing list of your discoveries. This may be time consuming, but it's fascinating! You may want to share this list with your SOAR group.

SEEK GOD – Week Five
Know God through Prayer
SHARE!

Week Four Review Question: Which activity did you choose? Tell how it impacted your understanding of God as Creator.

Objective: To seek to know God through prayer

Memory Verse:

> For the eyes of the Lord are on the righteous and his ears are attentive to their prayer. (1 Peter 3:12)

Why We Fail to Pray

> *"Your prayer for someone may or may not change them, but it always changes YOU."*
>
> — Craig Groeschel

Watch the prayer video.

What is prayer? It is communication with God. It is like picking up the phone to call a parent or a friend to share exciting news or a painful day. But with God, you never get a busy signal or voicemail. You don't have to wait for Him to call you back.

Communication with God can just start with simple, short conversations.

What are some of the reasons why people fail to pray?

Here are some reasons I (Sheri) fail to pray:

- I can get bored when it feels like I'm the only one talking.
- I am not really sure how to pray sometimes.
- I am distracted easily, and sometimes I actually forget that I am praying.
- I assume that God has more important things on which to spend His time.
- I reason that my prayers won't make a difference.

Levels of Prayer

There are levels of prayer based on your relationship with the Father. You can relate it to a friendship. When you first meet a friend, you might only see him or her occasionally or talk on the phone, but as your friendship grows, you increase your time together.

As we grow in knowing God as our Father and as our intimacy with Him increases, our prayer life should follow.

Everyone has a different relationship with God because we are unique individuals. Isn't it cool that God made, and loves, our individuality?

Prayer Progression

- **Simply talk to God.** You don't have to pray a wordy, reverent prayer. You can just say, "*Hi, God. Thank you for today.*"

- **Get real.** Be transparent. If you are mad, tell God about it. After I lost my mom, I would cry out, "*I am so sad, God. My heart is just broken. I miss my mom so much. I am sad that I will never have the relationship with her that I always longed to have.*"

- **Kneeling prayers** – Get on your knees in reverence.

- **Arrow prayers** – These are just short, anywhere prayers that lift up what is on your heart at that moment—while driving, cooking, working, or talking with others.

- **Eat Carpet prayers** – Get to the lowest possible place to pray to the Most High God. I ate a lot of carpet when my mom died.

- **Pray always.** I like open conversation with God. When I wake up, I pray and keep the line open all day. It's like when you call a company and they place you on hold for seven minutes, and then again for four more. I don't know about you, but I set the phone to speaker while I am waiting. When you finish just start again, it is like putting God on the speaker button.

- **Fasting prayers** – Withhold food (or something else) for a period of time and use the time you would have normally spent eating (or doing whatever else) in prayer. Or use your hunger pangs to remind you to pray for something that you are really seeking God about (Matthew 17:21 and Mark 9:29 KJV).

- **Scripture prayers** – God's Word never returns void. If you don't know what to pray, pray the Word. Our family loves to pray Ephesians 1:17-20 together.

- **In Jesus' Name prayers** – Ask in Jesus' name and then speak to the mountain in Jesus' name (Mark 11:20-26).

- **Spirit prayers** – When you don't know what to pray, ask God for the gift of praying in tongues, and pray "in the Spirit."

  > "But you, dear friends, build yourselves up in your most holy faith and pray in the Holy Spirit." (Jude 1:20)

GROUP SHARE TIME

- Why do you fail to pray? *forget: just don't think about it in the busy day to day*
- How real or transparent are you with God? Be honest. Rate yourself on a scale of 1-10 (10 being most real). *very real* *10* "He knows every thought before it comes from your lips" (Psalm 139).
- Today, with whom are you most real/transparent? *friends/family*

What do you want your prayer life to look like in one year? Get a vision for it! (Remember, where there is no vision, the people perish.) *Stronger*

Read Ephesians 1:17-22 and 3:16-20.

Paul prayed the following scriptures for believers. Pray these together and at home. Print and post these where you will see them throughout the week to remind you to pray them. God will change you from the inside out!

Ephesians 1:17-22

Father God of our Lord Jesus Christ, the Father of glory, that You may grant me a spirit of wisdom and revelation in the deep and intimate knowledge of You, By having the eyes of my heart flooded with light, so that I can know and understand the hope to which You have called me, and how rich is Your glorious inheritance in the saints.

And so that I can know and understand what is the immeasurable and unlimited and surpassing greatness of Your power in and for me and all those who believe, as demonstrated in the working of Your mighty strength, Which You exerted in Christ when You raised Christ from the dead and seated Him at Your [own] right hand in the heavens, Far above all rule and authority and power and dominion and every name that is named, not only in this age and in this world, but also in the age and the world which are to come.

And You have put all things under Your feet and have appointed Christ the universal and supreme Head of the church Which is His body, the fullness of Him Who fills all in all [for in that body lives the full measure of Him Who makes everything complete, and Who fills everything everywhere with Himself].

I pray this, waiting expectantly on You, Father, my God who watches over His word to perform it! In Jesus' Name, Amen.

Ephesians 3:16-20

Father, may You grant me out of the rich treasury of Your glory to be strengthened and reinforced with mighty power in the inner man by the [Holy] Spirit. May Christ through my faith [actually] dwell (make His permanent home) in my heart! May I be rooted deep in love and founded securely on love, That I may have the power and be strong to apprehend and grasp with all the saints what is the breadth and length and height and depth [of it]; That I may really come to know the love of Christ, which far surpasses mere knowledge; that you may be filled unto all the fullness of God [may have the richest measure of the divine Presence, and become a body wholly filled and flooded with God Himself].

Now to You, Lord who, by the power that is at work within me, is able to do superabundantly, far over and above all that we [dare] ask or think or imagine. To You be the glory in the church and in Christ Jesus throughout all generations forever and ever. Amen (so be it).

I pray this, waiting expectantly on You Father, my God who watches over His word to perform it! In Jesus' name, Amen.

SEEK GOD – Week Five
Know God through Prayer
EAT!

Objective: To seek to know God through prayer

Memory Verse:

> For the eyes of the Lord are on the righteous and his ears are attentive to their prayer. (1 Peter 3:12)

We can become more intimate with our Heavenly Father by seeking Him through prayer. I (Amy) used to look at prayer as something you do when you have an important request or a plea for help when tragedy strikes. Years ago I became aware of my prayerlessness when I realized how much my husband was praying. He would be sitting quietly in a chair and I would ask, "What you are doing?" His response was almost always, "Praying." I realized then that I didn't have a prayer life like that!

Thus I began my prayer journey. I wanted to have an authentic and dynamic relationship with my God through prayer. Now, after many years of focused effort and practice, prayer is a vital part of my entire life. Do you want this, too? You can experience God in such a close way that often it will seem that you've just spent time with your best friend. Whether you're a beginner or a prayer warrior, I pray that the next three weeks will move you into a deeper fellowship with God, the Lover of your soul.

Remember, faith is not a feeling, so if you do not feel like you are having an encounter with a best friend, do not worry. Relationships take time. Keep pressing toward the goal of getting to know Him!

Day 1   Why Pray

Read these verses on the importance of prayer.

> On the Sabbath we went outside the city gate to the river, where we expected to find a place of prayer. (Acts 16:13)

> Never be lacking in zeal, but keep your spiritual fervor, serving the Lord. Be joyful in hope, patient in affliction, faithful in prayer. (Romans 12:11-12)

Devote yourselves to prayer, being watchful and thankful. (Colossians 4:2)

For the eyes of the Lord are on the righteous and his ears are attentive to their prayer. (1 Peter 3:12)

God hears our prayers, and He wants us to pray. Have you ever thought, "Why do I pray if God already knows what I need before I ask? I've thought this many times! Yet prayer is important to God. He tells us to devote ourselves to it. It may be that you need a new mind-set about prayer. Don't miss this: first and foremost, we must look at prayer as a way to connect in fellowship with our Holy Father. Too often prayers are just a rote and scheduled part of certain events—mealtime, bedtime, the beginning of a sporting event, or the start or end of a Christian meeting. Frequently prayer is just something that we do when our loved ones or we have problems or crisis. Oh, how we miss out on the love relationship that the Father desires with us, when we only come to Him with our needs and rituals! Prayer can, and should be, the most relationally intimate time you have. Seek Him. Love Him. Know Him—in prayer.

Schedule some time today (maybe several times today) and go to a quiet place to be still before Him. Don't worry about your words until you've quieted your mind and turned your heart fully to Him. Quieting might take a while at first because we live at such a busy pace. You might try kneeling or any position that will help you focus and be authentic. Express your love to God. Delight yourself in Him: we are to find our pleasure in God. So many of us find our pleasures in the things of this world, but only God can truly satisfy our thirsty, hungry souls.

> *"Give me six hours to chop down a tree and I will spend the first four sharpening the axe."*
>
> — Abraham Lincoln

Day 2   No More Formulas

Read Matthew 6:5-24.

Get out your SOAR notebook and write out your favorite verse, then express what it means to you. You might want to write the "Five P's of Prayer" from the Lord's Prayer in your notebook. They are:

- **Presence** – Prayer should begin with the acknowledgment of God's Presence and an exclamation of who He is. (*Our Father in Heaven, Holy is Your name!*)
- **Priorities** – Our hearts need to be aligned with God's will in and for our lives. (*Your will be done on earth.*)
- **Provision** – We can ask God for His provision to meet all of our needs. (*Give us our daily bread*).
- **Pardon** – Pardon is giving to others the same forgiveness that Christ has given us. (*Forgive our debts as we forgive our debtors.*)

- **Power** – Pray for God's power to protect us from temptation and evil. (*Lead us not into temptation, but deliver us from evil.*)

Do your prayers include any of the "Five P's" listed above? Our prayers do not need to have formulas for them to be effective and meaningful. God wants prayers to come from the sincerity of our hearts. Jesus gave us the Lord's Prayer as a guide. I'm so thankful for this beautiful example of prayer. Aren't you?

Day 3   Repent Rebellion

Read Nehemiah 1.

This is an excellent passage about repentance. Allow God, through the Holy Spirit, to reveal to you areas of rebellion or blind spots that have not yet been transformed by the truth. Consider writing down what God reveals to you. Repent and ask Him to refine you as silver and gold. Keep praying in your quiet place.

Day 4   Take Hold

Read Genesis 32:24-32.

Jacob wrestled in prayer: "There is no one who calls on Your name, who arouses himself to take hold of You" (Isaiah 64:7). May this statement never be true of us! I desperately desire to "take hold of God" in prayer!

Matthew Henry Commentary gives us some more insight about Jacob's night of prayer. It states:

> "We are told by the prophet Hosea (Hosea 12:4) how Jacob wrestled: he wept, and made supplication; prayers and tears were his weapons. It was not only a physical, but a *spiritual wrestling*, by the vigorous acting of faith and holy desire; and thus all the spiritual seed of Jacob (all believers) that pray, in praying, still wrestle with God."

Jacob's name was changed to Israel that night in battle. Israel means "he who strives with God" or "he who perseveres." Also, the name Israel suggests royalty and power. This is not surprising since believers are a royal priesthood and we are called to persevere in our faith. Look at this verse in 1 Peter 2:9: "But you are a chosen people, a royal priesthood, a holy nation, a people belonging to God, that you may declare the praises of him who called you out of darkness into his wonderful light."

Let's realize today and forever that we can and should strive to "take hold" of God in prayer.

Day 5   Pray

Read the following scriptures:

> Be joyful always; pray continually; give thanks in all circumstances, for this is God's will for you in Christ Jesus. (1 Thessalonians 5:16)

> The end of all things is near. Therefore be clear-minded and self-controlled so that you can pray. (1 Peter 4:7)

Today do God's will and pray.

CRAVE

Read, pray, or meditate on these passages this week:

Psalm 86:1-13; 2 Chronicles 7:13-16; John 17.

SEEK GOD – Week Six
Know God through Prayer
SHARE!

Week Five Review Question: Share how your prayer time has changed since last week.

Objective: To seek to know God through prayer while resting, listening, and delighting in His presence

Memory Verse:

> Be still, and know that I am God; I will be exalted among the nations, I will be exalted in the earth. (Psalm 46:10)

Watch this week's video.

It is very difficult for me (Sheri) to be quiet! There are so many distractions that divide my attention: work, children, television, other people, sports, and so on. Maybe you are a person who is a skilled listener, or—like me—maybe you are the one who never stops talking long enough to listen.

When I am busy, distracted, talking, or formulating a response, I cannot possibly listen and truly hear others. The same is true when we are trying to hear from the Lord. He is gentle and kind. To hear Him, we need to learn the art of listening. We need to be still, intentionally, and wait on the Lord.

1. Can you tell the difference between what's going on in your head and God's voice?

2. Have you heard from the Lord before? If so, when do you typically hear from God? I've heard many people say, "In the shower." Why? Because in the shower we are still and there are no other distractions.

I remember a time when I had no idea how to discern my ideas from God's. I would say things like, "Is this God or is this me?" I was such a busy person that I didn't know God's voice because I was never still.

If you haven't ever known how to hear from the Lord, do not be discouraged: this is the right study for you!

GROUP SHARE TIME

Consider sharing methods that you use to slow down. Today in our groups, we will stop the distractions, be still, and spend time with the Father.

INDIVIDUAL SEEK TIME

Find a private place to be still; dwell on God, His presence, His names (from Week Three), or a scripture (some are listed below); pray; or just rest in Him. Decide how you would like to spend your time.

Scriptures

> The Lord is my shepherd, I shall not be in want. He makes me lie down in green pastures, he leads me beside quiet waters, he restores my soul. He guides me in paths of righteousness for his name's sake. (Psalm 23:1-3)

If you are not experiencing periods of rest, maybe you should ask, "God, am I missing it?"

> "My people will live in peaceful dwelling places, in secure homes, in undisturbed places of rest. Take my yoke upon you and learn from me, for I am gentle and humble in heart, and you will find rest for your souls." (Matthew 11:28-29)

Are you at rest? I am not talking about the sleeping kind of rest but an inexplicable peacefulness in your soul? I (Sheri) lost my mom to cancer in 2006. I grieved and missed her so much; but even with all of the pain, I had a peace in my soul that could not be explained in words.

NOW SHARE!

Gather back together. Share how this quiet time ministered to you. How is God transforming you in your relationship with Him?

Celebrate and pray for each another.

SEEK GOD – Week Six
Know God through Prayer
EAT!

Objective: Seeking to know God through prayer while resting, listening, and delighting in His presence

Memory Verse:

> Be still, and know that I am God; I will be exalted among the nations, I will be exalted in the earth. (Psalm 46:10)

Is your life anything like mine? My (Amy's) life is really busy! I have *seven* people (spouse included!) to pour into spiritually, provide nutritious meals for, engage in meaningful conversations, and nurse when they are injured or sick. I manage a home that requires repairs and cleaning. Can anyone say ... laundry?! I also have the privilege to home-educate my six kids. Regardless of lifestyle, we all need recharging!

What you and I need is not chill time in front of the tube. More than anything else, we need a quiet place to be still and reflect on the God who made us and gave us life.

Prayer is very important! Many find it hard to spend time in extended prayer. Is it because we are too busy or because we do not deem prayer important enough to fit into our plans?

Do you want to know God more intimately? Do you want God to speak to you and show you His path for you? I sure do! Who's with me?

This week we're going to learn and practice the skill of resting and listening.

Give your whole self (spirit, soul, and body) to knowing and loving your wonderful Savior.

Day 1   Righteous One

Read Psalm 37.

There's a lot to chew on in this chapter, including thoughts on "delighting" and "being still." What does it say about the Righteous? That's *you*. It's hard to believe, isn't it? But it's true! Christ in you produces your righteousness.

Pull out your notebook and ask yourself these questions from your reading:

- What is your favorite verse? Why? Consider committing it to memory.
- Which verse was confusing? We all get confused sometimes. Just be real with God and ask Him to help you understand.
- Does any verse challenge you or bring a deeper understanding of God? How can this verse change you this week?

Day 2   Ears to Hear

Read John 10 today.

> It was at this time that He (Jesus) went off to the mountain to pray, and He spent the whole night in prayer to God. (Luke 6:12)

Ask God to speak to you. Ask God to unclog your spiritual ears. Listen for the Holy Spirit's voice. God wants us to live "as Christ"—to be alert always and spiritually sensitive to His guiding and gentle voice. It would be a major blessing to write down the verses from John 10 that you find most memorable.

Day 3   Quick to Listen

Read James 1:19-25.

Be quick to listen and slow to speak. Listening isn't processing information or preparing a response. It is simply receiving. If we don't listen well, how can we get our instructions from God? Listening intentionally allows us to receive all that God has for us.

We are called to be totally surrendered to God. Jim Elliot, in his book *Shadow of the Almighty*, said, "One does not surrender a life in an instant; that which is lifelong can only be surrendered in a lifetime."

Do you trust God? I didn't for a long time, and today there are still areas in which I probably depend on myself more than I place my trust in God. Read these verses and strive with me to surrender and trust Him fully.

> Trust in the Lord with all your heart and do not lean on your own understanding. In all your ways acknowledge Him, and He will make your paths straight. (Proverbs 3:5-6)

Be anxious for nothing, but in everything by prayer and supplication with thanksgiving let your requests be made known to God. And the peace of God, which surpasses all comprehension, will guard your hearts and your minds in Christ Jesus. (Philippians 4:6-7)

Day 4   Meditate

Read Psalm 5, 130, and 131.

As you sit and meditate on this, turn your whole heart and mind to God and be still before Him. Let Him quiet your soul and give you rest, peace, and comfort.

Write in your notebook how, today, you will apply one or more of these verses in your life.

Day 5   Fight for You

Ask God for insight as you read Exodus 14.

Describe in your own words what verse 14 means to you.

We serve a mighty God! Did verse 14 stand out to you: "The Lord will fight for you; you need only to be still"? Our LORD will fight all your battles! Your job is to pray (ask), wait on Him (be still), and walk in trust and faith (total reliance upon Him).

Have you ever fought your own battle by defending yourself against others? I don't know about you, but when I have done this, I always end up feeling bad and it never results in changing someone else's opinion of me. My way can seem right and feel like the most immediate path to resolution, but what's right in my mind is not necessarily God's way.

Remember, God is your defender! If He is for you, who can be against you?

Today ask God to help you learn to stand firm while resting in Him. He will care for you in your battles!

You might consider writing your own prayer to your Father God. Listen. Respond. Rejoice. He is faithful!

CRAVE

Read Proverbs 8. This chapter in Proverbs is about Wisdom (which is Christ, according to some commentators). Read 2 Corinthians 12:7-10 and Hebrews 3, which is about Israel's stubborn unbelief and unwillingness to listen.

SEEK GOD – Week Seven
Know God through Prayer
SHARE!

Week Six Review Question: Did you write a note to God in your prayer journal this week? If so, would you share it with us?

Objective: Seeking to know God through intercessory prayer, petitions, and faith

Memory Verse:

> And pray in the Spirit on all occasions with all kinds of prayers and requests. (Ephesians 6:18)

Today we have the opportunity to pray together! Some of you might be really comfortable with this. For others, this might be your first time, and you might have the desire to run for the door—but don't! I (Sheri) remember the first time I had to pray aloud with others. I was scared! I have no idea what words came out of my mouth, but I know the prayer was short.

Don't worry about what you sound like or about what you say or don't say. Remember that what God wants most of all is *you*. He wants a relationship with you. You don't have a relationship if you don't talk to or spend time with God.

Jesus' last words in John 17 were that the Body of Christ would be one as He and the Father were one. Coming together in prayer is a strategic way to exercise unity. It will build you up and help you pray on the spot with others in the future.

GROUP SHARE! TIME

Read this passage together.

> Finally, be strong in the Lord and in his mighty power. Put on the full armor of God so that you can take your stand against the devil's schemes. For our struggle is not against flesh and blood, but against the rulers, against the authorities, against the powers of this dark world and against the spiritual forces of evil in the heavenly realms. Therefore put on the full armor of God, so that when the day of evil comes, you may be able to stand your ground, and after you have done everything, to

stand. Stand firm then, with the belt of truth buckled around your waist, with the breastplate of righteousness in place, and with your feet fitted with the readiness that comes from the gospel of peace. In addition to all this, take up the shield of faith, with which you can extinguish all the flaming arrows of the evil one. Take the helmet of salvation and the sword of the Spirit, which is the word of God. And pray in the Spirit on all occasions with all kinds of prayers and requests. With this in mind, be alert and always keep on praying for all the saints. (Ephesians 6:10-18)

What stands out to you in these verses? One thing that stands out to me is that we are in a spiritual battle. Can you see the "Spirit world?" I can't. So many times I try to fight the battles that I can see with my eyes, but there are other things going on within the spiritual realm that I cannot see. Prayer is a weapon in this battle!

Like we shared with you on the video this week, share with one another the journey of your personal prayer life and relationship with God.

Now break into prayer partnerships, and let's pray with one another. Be real and transparent with God. Don't feel intimidated about sharing your heart with God in front of someone else. Don't worry about what you sound like or about what you say or don't say. Just allow yourself to be vulnerable with God.

What if you don't know what to pray? The Bible is packed full of prayers. Jeremiah 1:12 says that God's Word is active and alive and that He watches over the Word to perform it; so you can never go wrong praying Scripture.

Here are some scriptural prayers that you may want to keep with you to pray when needed:

- For protection (Psalm 91)
- To know God, your calling, identity and what is yours (Ephesians 1:17-23)
- To deepen your understanding of God (Ephesians 3:16-20)
- To understand that God knows your thoughts (Psalm 139:1-4)
- When your mountain (your problems or circumstances) seems too enormous (Isaiah 41:15 and Mark 11:23)

SHARE NOW!

Gather back together. Discuss why prayer is important to you.

SEEK GOD – Week Seven
Know God through Prayer
EAT!

Objective: Seeking to know God through intercessory prayer, petitions, and faith

Memory Verse:

> And pray in the Spirit on all occasions with all kinds of prayers and requests. (Ephesians 6:18)

In 2007 my (Amy's) prayer life took a huge turn for the better. I had been walking with God for nearly 20 years; the trouble was that I had become a professional (or so I thought) Christian. God was in a neat and tidy box that I had made out of "good" theology. Please don't misunderstand. If God's Word could be called "the box," then that is the box in which we all can safely abide. My box had forgotten, left out, or misplaced the truth that our prayers can, by faith, move mountains!

Also, I rediscovered that a person abiding in Christ and living out of His righteousness has an advantage. James 5 tells us, "The prayer of a *righteous* man is powerful and effective." All Christians are positionally righteous, but not all live out of that righteousness. Therefore, my prayers can be hindered by unconfessed, unsurrendered sin. God is speaking to the unclogged ears of the righteous! He's listening, too. Are you listening? Are you making your requests? Are you interceding?

Basically, in my life, my box blew up! I took the limits off of God, and He became infinitely greater to me. And I am more acutely aware of His power working in and through me.

Prayer is one of the greatest privileges that a believer has on this earth. Through prayer we gain access to the greatest power source known to man—God Almighty. You have an opportunity now to read, look closely at, soak in, take seriously, receive, and believe the following scriptures. Do you want to become a person of prayer and faith? Better yet, do you want to have effective and powerful prayers? If you give yourself to the quest of seeking to understand prayer better, this will be a faith-building, life-changing time for you! Ask the Holy Spirit to teach and guide you as you study.

You may want to order and begin reading a book on prayer that I (Amy) highly recommend, *The Kneeling Christian* by an Unknown Author (published by Zondervan). My desire is that you will know God intimately through prayer, rest in Him, and believe like you've never believed before that "with God *all* things are possible!" Please understand that these verses are not meant to be formulas for us to use to get what we want. I see them as our calling, as believers, to believe God at His Word.

When we do all that we can, praying in faith, then we must rest with assurance that the end results are in His hands. Sin has brought tremendous suffering into our world. But God, in His love and mercy, works *everything* out for good for the beloved and called.

Day 1   Prayer Attitude

"Answered prayer is the interchange of love between the Father and His child."
— Andrew Murray

There are seven days of assignments this week. You may want to spend the next two weeks studying and meditating on these passages.

Here are some ideas for your study time: Read, read, and re-read the Scriptures. Document in your SOAR notebook all that stands out to you. You will see how closely prayer and faith are related. "Faith comes from hearing and hearing the word of God" (Romans 10:17).

> Is any one of you in trouble? He should pray. Is anyone happy? Let him sing songs of praise. Is any one of you sick? He should call the elders of the church to pray over him and anoint him with oil in the name of the Lord. And the prayer offered in faith will make the sick person well; the Lord will raise him up. If he has sinned, he will be forgiven. Therefore confess your sins to each other and pray for each other so that you may be healed. The prayer of a righteous man is powerful and effective. Elijah was a man just like us. He prayed earnestly that it would not rain, and it did not rain on the land for three and a half years. Again he prayed, and the heavens gave rain, and the earth produced its crops. (James 5:13-18)

Do you confess your sins to other believers?

All sins were paid for on the cross. However, when you are living in a way that is disobedient and doesn't honor God, the Holy Spirit will convict you of this. If you continue to live in sin as a believer, you leave a door open for the enemy (Satan) to enter and attack, and you live outside of the umbrella of protection that God has set out for you. Confess your sins quickly to one another because a sin in the dark has power over you but a sin brought into the light can set you free! We are children of the Light.

> If any of you lacks wisdom, he should ask God, who gives generously to all without finding fault, and it will be given to him. But when he asks, he must believe and not doubt, because he who doubts is like a wave of the sea, blown and tossed by the wind. That man should not think he will receive anything from the Lord; he is a double-minded man, unstable in all he does. (James 1:5-8 KJV)

Have you ever felt like "...a wave of the sea, blown and tossed by the wind?" I know that I (Sheri) have! I remember when there was no peace in my life. I would ask God for something, but if I were honest with you, I would admit that I didn't really believe that He would do it.

Pray the Ephesians 1:17-23 prayer from Week Five, and ask God to grant you a spirit of wisdom and revelation. I have prayed this prayer for more than four years. I can testify that God has truly flooded the eyes of my heart to understand and believe His Word.

According to the following passage, what should be your attitude when you pray? Write notes as you read along. This will help to reinforce what you are learning.

Now He was telling them a parable to show that at all times they ought to pray and not to lose heart, saying, "There was in a certain city a judge who did not fear God, and did not respect man. And there was a widow in that city, and she kept coming to him, saying, 'Give me legal protection from my opponent.' And for a while he was unwilling; but afterward he said to himself, 'Even though I do not fear God nor respect man, yet because this widow bothers me, I will give her legal protection, lest by continually coming she wear me out.'" And the Lord said, "Hear what the unrighteous judge said; now shall not God bring about justice for His elect, who cry to Him day and night, and will He delay long over them? I tell you that He will bring about justice for them speedily. However, when the Son of Man comes, will He find faith on the earth?"

And He also told this parable to certain ones who trusted in themselves that they were righteous, and viewed others with contempt: "Two men went up into the temple to pray, one a Pharisee, and the other a tax-gatherer. The Pharisee stood and was praying thus to himself, 'God, I thank Thee that I am not like other people: swindlers, unjust, adulterers, or even like this tax-gatherer. I fast twice a week; I pay tithes of all that I get.' But the tax-gatherer, standing some distance away, was even unwilling to lift up his eyes to heaven, but was beating his breast, saying, 'God, be merciful to me, the sinner!' I tell you, this man went down to his house justified rather than the other; for everyone who exalts himself shall be humbled, but he who humbles himself shall be exalted." And they were bringing even their babies to Him so that He might touch them, but when the disciples saw it, they began rebuking them. But Jesus called for them, saying, "Permit the children to come to Me, and do not hinder them, for the kingdom of God belongs to such as these. Truly I say to you, whoever does not receive the kingdom of God like a child shall not enter it at all." (Luke 18:1-17 NASB)

Day 2   With Faith

Are you ready for another day of seeking God? Pause and prepare your heart to receive from His holy Word...

The word "faith" is used more than 250 times in the New Testament. Our faith is paramount! Here's one verse that really stands out to me: "And without faith it is impossible to please God" (Hebrews 11:6 KJV).

Stop! Read that again and let it soak in. Another powerful verse states in Romans 14:23 that "everything that does not come from faith is sin." The Holy Spirit has convicted me several times regarding my lack of faith in different situations. Now let's read about Peter's faith:

> In Joppa there was a disciple named Tabitha (which, when translated, is Dorcas), who was always doing good and helping the poor. About that time she became sick and died, and her body was washed and placed in an upstairs room. Lydda was near Joppa; so when the disciples heard that Peter was in Lydda, they sent two men to him and urged him, "Please come at once!"
>
> Peter went with them, and when he arrived he was taken upstairs to the room. All the widows stood around him, crying and showing him the robes and other clothing that Dorcas had made while she was still with them. Peter sent them all out of the room; then he got down on his knees and prayed. Turning toward the dead woman, he said, "Tabitha, get up." She opened her eyes, and seeing Peter she sat up. He took her by the hand and helped her to her feet. Then he called the believers and the widows and presented her to them alive. This became known all over Joppa, and many people believed in the Lord. Peter stayed in Joppa for some time with a tanner named Simon. (Acts 9:36-43 KJV)

I love this passage! He got on His knees and prayed. Next he spoke to Tabitha (see also Mark 11:23). He prayed, believed, and believed it so much that he spoke to a dead person, knowing that God would give him what he had prayed for. He wasn't shocked at the power of God because He knew God. Do you desire faith in God like Peter's? I do! "Let us fix our eyes on Jesus, the author and perfecter of our faith…" (Hebrew 12:2).

So, are you stuck with the same measure of faith? Check out these scriptures and ask God to strengthen and increase your faith in Him.

> We ought always to thank God for you, brothers, and rightly so, because your faith is growing more and more, and the love every one of you has for each other is increasing. Therefore, among God's churches we boast about your perseverance and faith in all the persecutions and trials you are enduring. (2 Thessalonians 1:3-4)
>
> Then one of the crowd answered and said, "Teacher, I brought You my son, who has a mute spirit. And wherever it seizes him, it throws him down; he foams at the mouth, gnashes his teeth, and becomes rigid. So I spoke to Your disciples, that they should cast it out, but they could not." He answered him and said, "O faithless generation, how long shall I be with you? How long shall I bear with you? Bring him to Me." Then they brought him to Him. And when he saw Him, immediately the spirit convulsed him, and he fell on the ground and wallowed, foaming at the mouth. So He asked his father,

"How long has this been happening to him?" And he said, "From childhood. And often he has thrown him both into the fire and into the water to destroy him. But if You can do anything, have compassion on us and help us." Jesus said to him, "If you can believe, all things are possible to him who believes." Immediately the father of the child cried out and said with tears, "Lord, I believe; help my unbelief!" When Jesus saw that the people came running together, He rebuked the unclean spirit, saying to it, "Deaf and dumb spirit, I command you, come out of him and enter him no more!" Then the spirit cried out, convulsed him greatly, and came out of him. And he became as one dead, so that many said, "He is dead." But Jesus took him by the hand and lifted him up, and he arose. And when He had come into the house, His disciples asked Him privately, "Why could we not cast it out?" So He said to them, "This kind can come out by nothing but prayer and fasting." (Mark 9:17-29 NKJV)

Pull out your SOAR notebook. We have been through many scriptures today.

- Write down your favorite verse from this passage.
- Which verse shook you up or challenged you to know and seek God more?

Day 3   Prepared Heart

Prepare your heart by asking God to reveal His truth to you.

The next day as they were leaving Bethany, Jesus was hungry. Seeing in the distance a fig tree in leaf, he went to find out if it had any fruit. When he reached it, he found nothing but leaves, because it was not the season for figs. Then he said to the tree, "May no one ever eat fruit from you again." And his disciples heard him say it. On reaching Jerusalem, Jesus entered the temple area and began driving out those who were buying and selling there. He overturned the tables of the money changers and the benches of those selling doves, and would not allow anyone to carry merchandise through the temple courts. And as he taught them, he said, "Is it not written: 'My house will be called a house of prayer for all nations?' But you have made it a den of robbers." The chief priests and the teachers of the law heard this and began looking for a way to kill him, for they feared him, because the whole crowd was amazed at his teaching.

When evening came, they went out of the city. In the morning, as they went along, they saw the fig tree withered from the roots. Peter remembered and said to Jesus, "Rabbi, look! The fig tree you cursed has withered!" "Have faith in God," Jesus answered. "I tell you the truth, if anyone says to this mountain, 'Go, throw yourself into the sea,' and does not doubt in his heart but believes that what he says will happen, it will be done for him. Therefore I tell you, whatever you ask for in prayer, believe that you have received it, and it will be yours. And when you stand praying, if you hold anything against anyone, forgive him, so that your Father in heaven may forgive you your sins." (Mark 11:12-25 KJV)

Jesus made some amazing statements about faith. Is there anything too difficult for God, the One who created everything? Recently a friend of our family (Amy's) was diagnosed with colon cancer. The doctors said it was terminal and that he only had six months to live. This friend witnessed to the doctor and told him that he believed that God would heal him. He later prayed and told God that he wanted God to be amazed by his faith. Guess what? Yep! This dear friend was totally healed— in a matter of weeks! The doctor was amazed. American Christians do not always experience the miraculous power of God as other believers from around the world do. Could it be that we have God in a box? Do we limit God?

What mountains are in your life?

Consider this: prayer without faith is useless.

> What good is it, my brothers, if a man claims to have faith but has no deeds? Can such faith save him? Suppose a brother or sister is without clothes and daily food. If one of you says to him, "Go, I wish you well; keep warm and well fed," but does nothing about his physical needs, what good is it? In the same way, faith by itself, if it is not accompanied by action, is dead. But someone will say, "You have faith; I have deeds." Show me your faith without deeds, and I will show you my faith by what I do. You believe that there is one God. Good! Even the demons believe that—and shudder. You foolish man, do you want evidence that faith without deeds is useless? Was not our ancestor Abraham considered righteous for what he did when he offered his son Isaac on the altar? You see that his faith and his actions were working together, and his faith was made complete by what he did. And the scripture was fulfilled that says, "Abraham believed God, and it was credited to him as righteousness," and he was called God's friend. You see that a person is justified by what he does and not by faith alone. In the same way, was not even Rahab the prostitute considered righteous for what she did when she gave lodging to the spies and sent them off in a different direction? As the body without the spirit is dead, so faith without deeds is dead. (James 2:14-3:1)

How do you live out your faith? Living in obedience to God is faith in action!

If you say you believe, but your actions don't match, then maybe you only have knowledge of God. We can have knowledge of God without having faith (trust and reliance upon Him). Stop for a minute and evaluate where you are.

Now read these scriptures for an understanding of true salvation:

> For by grace you have been saved through faith; and that not of yourselves, it is the gift of God; not as a result of works, that no one should boast. For we are His workmanship, created in Christ Jesus for good works, which God prepared beforehand, that we should walk in them. (Ephesians 2:8-10 NASB)

We are given faith as a gift from God. Yet take note of this: faith is not stagnant. Faith can be strengthened and weakened. Look at how we soar with faith in the text below:

> So then faith cometh by hearing, and hearing by the word of God.
> (Romans 10:17 KJV)

Our faith can increase! Isn't it marvelous that God provided a way for us to increase our faith—by hearing His Word? As you renew your mind with the Word of God, faith will result.

Pray this prayer:

> *Father, I pray right now that you transform the innermost parts of my mind and heart through the power of your Holy Spirit and renew my mind with Your Word! Strengthen my faith. I want to have enormous faith in you. In Jesus' name, amen.*

Day 4   Present

Stop and spend some time in prayer before you read today. Acknowledge His presence with you.

> Therefore, since we have a great high priest who has gone through the heavens, Jesus the Son of God, let us hold firmly to the faith we profess. For we do not have a high priest who is unable to sympathize with our weaknesses, but we have one who has been tempted in every way, just as we are-yet was without sin. Let us then approach the throne of grace with confidence, so that we may receive mercy and find grace to help us in our time of need. (Hebrews 4:14-16)

I (Sheri) cannot tell you how much of my Christian walk I spent going to the throne of condemnation (or so I thought). I just couldn't seem to get control of my mouth or my behavior. I would drag myself to the throne, full of guilt and pain in my heart for my lack of ability to walk in the truth. I never felt that I was worthy to ask for anything of magnitude. I didn't realize that it was the *throne of grace*. You and I can approach God in prayer with confidence—as a son or daughter of a loving Father and the King of Kings!

Now grab your SOAR notebook and take notes while you read these amazing verses:

Immediately Jesus made the disciples get into the boat and go on ahead of him to the other side, while he dismissed the crowd. After he had dismissed them, he went up on a mountainside by himself to pray. When evening came, he was there alone, but the boat was already a considerable distance from land, buffeted by the waves because the wind was against it. During the fourth watch of the night Jesus went out to them, walking on the lake. When the disciples saw him walking on the lake, they were terrified. "It's a ghost," they said, and cried out in fear. But Jesus immediately said to them: "Take courage! It is I. Don't be afraid." "Lord, if it's you," Peter replied, "tell me to come to you on the water." "Come," he said. Then Peter got down out of the boat, walked on the water and came toward Jesus. But when he saw the wind, he was afraid and, beginning to sink, cried out, "Lord, save me!" Immediately Jesus reached out his hand and caught him. "You of little faith," he said, "why did you doubt?" And when they climbed into the boat, the wind died down. Then those who were in the boat worshiped him, saying, "Truly you are the Son of God." (Matthew 14:22-33)

Has looking at your circumstances been a fire extinguisher to your faith? Faith is not a feeling. We have to keep our eyes on Jesus!

Coming to his hometown, he began teaching the people in their synagogue, and they were amazed. "Where did this man get this wisdom and these miraculous powers?" they asked. "Isn't this the carpenter's son? Isn't his mother's name Mary, and aren't his brothers James, Joseph, Simon and Judas? Aren't all his sisters with us? Where then did this man get all these things?" And they took offense at him. But Jesus said to them, "Only in his hometown and in his own house is a prophet without honor." And he did not do many miracles there because of their lack of faith. (Matthew 13:54-58)

Well-meaning Christian cultures can become faithless. Sometimes church and religious disciplines become too common—the norm. We become desensitized. That's when we have substituted religion for a dynamic faith relationship with God. Pray this with me (Amy): "*Father, I pray that we will know and want nothing but you.*"

Imagine what it felt like to Jesus, not to be able to minister fully in His hometown. He came and laid down His life for all of us—even those who rejected Him.

Just then a woman who had been subject to bleeding for twelve years came up behind him and touched the edge of his cloak. She said to herself, "If I only touch his cloak, I will be healed." Jesus turned and saw her. "Take heart, daughter," he said, "your faith has healed you." And the woman was healed from that moment. When

Jesus entered the ruler's house and saw the flute players and the noisy crowd, he said, "Go away. The girl is not dead but asleep." But they laughed at him. After the crowd had been put outside, he went in and took the girl by the hand, and she got up. News of this spread through all that region. As Jesus went on from there, two blind men followed him, calling out, "Have mercy on us, Son of David!" When he had gone indoors, the blind men came to him, and he asked them, "Do you believe that I am able to do this?" "Yes, Lord," they replied. Then he touched their eyes and said, "According to your faith will it be done to you"; and their sight was restored. Jesus warned them sternly, "See that no one knows about this." But they went out and spread the news about him all over that region. (Matthew 9:20-31)

- If you had to develop a statement to capture the essence of all of these verses' meanings, in ten words or less, what would that statement be? Write it down in your SOAR notebook.

- Which verse has impacted your life the most this week?

Day 5　Prayer in the Battle

When Jesus had entered Capernaum, a centurion came to him, asking for help. "Lord," he said, "my servant lies at home paralyzed and in terrible suffering." Jesus said to him, "I will go and heal him." The centurion replied, "Lord, I do not deserve to have you come under my roof. But just say the word, and my servant will be healed. For I myself am a man under authority, with soldiers under me. I tell this one, 'Go,' and he goes; and that one, 'Come,' and he comes. I say to my servant, 'Do this,' and he does it." When Jesus heard this, he was astonished and said to those following him, "I tell you the truth, I have not found anyone in Israel with such great faith. I say to you that many will come from the east and the west, and will take their places at the feast with Abraham, Isaac and Jacob in the kingdom of heaven. But the subjects of the kingdom will be thrown outside, into the darkness, where there will be weeping and gnashing of teeth." Then Jesus said to the centurion, "Go! It will be done just as you believed it would." And his servant was healed at that very hour. (Matthew 8:5-13)

Do you want Jesus to be astonished by your faith in Him?

Then he got into the boat and his disciples followed him. Without warning, a furious storm came up on the lake, so that the waves swept over the boat. But Jesus was sleeping. The disciples went and woke him, saying, "Lord, save us! We're going to drown!" He replied, "You of little faith, why are you so afraid?" Then he got up and rebuked the winds and the waves, and it was completely calm. The men were amazed and asked, "What kind of man is this? Even the winds and the waves obey him!" (Matthew 8:23-27)

Jesus was with them in the boat—yet they were still afraid! What storm is in your life right now? Maybe you are in a financial storm? A marital storm? The same Jesus who rebuked the storm in which the disciples were caught lives in you! What can you learn from these scriptures to build your prayer life and faith in Jesus?

Jesus could have told the disciples to ride out the storm because He was with them, but that is not what Jesus did. He rebuked the storm, and there was an immediate, perfect peace. He can do the same for you today. Pray and ask! He is the same today as He was in that boat all those years ago.

Now let's look at some Scripture about intercessory prayer.

> Epaphras, who is one of your number, a bondslave of Jesus Christ, sends you his greetings, always laboring earnestly for you in his prayers, that you may stand perfect and fully assured in all the will of God. (Colossians 4:12 NASB)

> We have not stopped praying for you and asking God to fill you with the knowledge of his will through all spiritual wisdom and understanding. And we pray this in order that you may live a life worthy of the Lord and may please him in every way: bearing fruit in every good work, growing in the knowledge of God, being strengthened with all power according to his glorious might so that you may have great endurance and patience, and joyfully giving thanks to the Father, who has qualified you to share in the inheritance of the saints in the kingdom of light. For he has rescued us from the dominion of darkness and brought us into the kingdom of the Son he loves, in whom we have redemption, the forgiveness of sins. (Colossians 1:9-14)

Wow! Have you ever prayed for the Body of Christ in a similar way? Before you continue, read those verses again and compile a list of what Paul asked God to do on behalf of his brothers and sisters in Christ. Ask God to stir you and motivate you to labor in intercessory prayer for the saints.

> Finally, be strong in the Lord and in his mighty power. Put on the full armor of God so that you can take your stand against the devil's schemes. For our struggle is not against flesh and blood, but against the rulers, against the authorities, against the powers of this dark world and against the spiritual forces of evil in the heavenly realms. Therefore put on the full armor of God, so that when the day of evil comes, you may be able to stand your ground, and after you have done everything, to stand. Stand firm then, with the belt of truth buckled around your waist, with the breastplate of righteousness in place, and with your feet fitted with the readiness

that comes from the gospel of peace. In addition to all this, take up the shield of faith, with which you can extinguish all the flaming arrows of the evil one. Take the helmet of salvation and the sword of the Spirit, which is the word of God. And pray in the Spirit on all occasions with all kinds of prayers and requests. With this in mind, be alert and always keep on praying for all the saints. (Ephesians 6:10-18)

Prayer is important because it is how we war in the spiritual battle.

- How have you been warring in the past? With prayer or with your own strength?
- How will you battle differently in the future?

Day 6   Pray in Agreement

"I am the true vine, and My Father is the vinedresser. Every branch in Me that does not bear fruit, He takes away; and every branch that bears fruit, He prunes it so that it may bear more fruit. You are already clean because of the word which I have spoken to you. Abide in Me, and I in you. As the branch cannot bear fruit of itself unless it abides in the vine, so neither can you unless you abide in Me. I am the vine, you are the branches; he who abides in Me and I in him, he bears much fruit, for apart from Me you can do nothing. If anyone does not abide in Me, he is thrown away as a branch and dries up; and they gather them, and cast them into the fire and they are burned. If you abide in Me, and My words abide in you, ask whatever you wish, and it will be done for you. My Father is glorified by this, that you bear much fruit, and so prove to be My disciples. Just as the Father has loved Me, I have also loved you; abide in My love. If you keep My commandments, you will abide in My love; just as I have kept My Father's commandments and abide in His love. These things I have spoken to you so that My joy may be in you, and that your joy may be made full. This is My commandment, that you love one another, just as I have loved you. Greater love has no one than this, that one lay down his life for his friends." (John 15:1-13 NASB)

Let's look at two parts of this passage: "*apart from me*" and "*If you abide.*" "Apart from me" means that apart from Him, it's impossible to be fruitful and our prayers are hindered. When we are abiding in the love of God, He makes us fruit bearers.

Answered prayer is about God's will and glory being accomplished on earth through us.

Now let's look at the fruitfulness of a believer who abides in the Vine!

"I tell you the truth, my Father will give you whatever you ask in my name. Until now you have not asked for anything in my name. Ask and you will receive, and your joy will be complete." (John 16:23-24)

"I tell you the truth, anyone who has faith in me will do what I have been doing. He will do even greater things than these, because I am going to the Father. And I will do whatever you ask in my name, so that the Son may bring glory to the Father. You may ask me for anything in my name, and I will do it." (John 14:12-14)

"Ask, and it will be given to you; seek, and you will find; knock, and it will be opened to you. For everyone who asks receives, and he who seeks finds, and to him who knocks it will be opened. Or what man is there among you who, when his son asks for a loaf, will give him a stone? Or if he asks for a fish, he will not give him a snake, will he? If you then, being evil, know how to give good gifts to your children, how much more will your Father who is in heaven give what is good to those who ask Him!" (Matthew 7:7-11 NASB)

"Truly I say to you, whatever you bind on earth shall have been bound in heaven; and whatever you loose on earth shall have been loosed in heaven. Again I say to you, that if two of you agree on earth about anything that they may ask, it shall be done for them by My Father who is in heaven. For where two or three have gathered together in My name, I am there in their midst." (Matthew 18:18-20 NASB)

Do you have someone to pray in agreement with you on a regular basis—a prayer partner? If not, consider asking God to show you who He wants to be your prayer partner. I (Amy) prayed this prayer a few years back. Not long after that, I had a name of an acquaintance pop into my mind with the thought she would be the perfect person to ask to be my prayer partner. I located her phone number, called her up, and then stumbled through trying to explain my reason for calling. Awkward!

Do you know what she said in response to my request? Basically she said, "I have chills. I have asked God for a prayer partner and He told me to wait because He would send her to me." Wow! God is so good and faithful.

Day 7   Enlist on God's Prayer Team

Today as you read the truth of God's Word, open your SOAR notebook and take notes on what each Scripture passage teaches about prayer. Look carefully. Remember that the Holy Spirit is your Teacher. Are you teachable? Tell God that you are hungry to know Him more and ask Him to make you teachable.

First of all, then, I urge that entreaties and prayers, petitions and thanksgivings, be made on behalf of all men, for kings and all who are in authority, so that we may lead a tranquil and quiet life in all godliness and dignity. This is good and acceptable in the sight of God our Savior, who desires all men to be saved and to come to the knowledge of the truth. [...] Therefore I want the men in every place to pray, lifting up holy hands, without wrath and dissension. (1 Timothy 2:1-4, 8 NASB)

Wives, likewise, be submissive to your own husbands, that even if some do not obey the word, they, without a word, may be won by the conduct of their wives, when they observe your chaste conduct accompanied by fear. Do not let your adornment be merely outward--arranging the hair, wearing gold, or putting on fine apparel-- rather let it be the hidden person of the heart, with the incorruptible beauty of a gentle and quiet spirit, which is very precious in the sight of God. For in this manner, in former times, the holy women who trusted in God also adorned themselves, being submissive to their own husbands, as Sarah obeyed Abraham, calling him lord, whose daughters you are if you do good and are not afraid with any terror. Husbands, likewise, dwell with them with understanding, giving honor to the wife, as to the weaker vessel, and as being heirs together of the grace of life, that your prayers may not be hindered. Finally, all of you be of one mind, having compassion for one another; love as brothers, be tenderhearted, be courteous; not returning evil for evil or reviling for reviling, but on the contrary blessing, knowing that you were called to this, that you may inherit a blessing. For He who would love life and see good days, Let him refrain his tongue from evil, And his lips from speaking deceit. Let him turn away from evil and do good; Let him seek peace and pursue it. For the eyes of the LORD are on the righteous, And His ears are open to their prayers; But the face of the LORD is against those who do evil. (1 Peter 3:1-12 NKJV)

The sacrifice of the wicked is an abomination to the LORD: but the prayer of the upright is his delight. (Proverbs 15:8 KJV)

Cornelius answered: "Four days ago I was in my house praying at this hour, at three in the afternoon. Suddenly a man in shining clothes stood before me and said, 'Cornelius, God has heard your prayer and remembered your gifts to the poor. Send to Joppa for Simon who is called Peter. He is a guest in the home of Simon the tanner, who lives by the sea.'" (Acts 10:30-33)

The Lord is near to all who call on him, to all who call on him in truth. He fulfills the desires of those who fear him; he hears their cry and saves them. (Psalm 145:18-19)

I cried to Him with my mouth, And He was extolled with my tongue. If I regard wickedness in my heart, The Lord will not hear; But certainly God has heard; He has given heed to the voice of my prayer. Blessed be God, Who has not turned away my prayer, nor His loving-kindness from me. (Psalm 66:17-20 NASB)

Because of the surpassing greatness of the revelations, for this reason, to keep me from exalting myself, there was given me a thorn in the flesh, a messenger of Satan to torment me—to keep me from exalting myself! Concerning this I implored the Lord three times that it might leave me. And He has said to me, "My grace is sufficient for you, for power is perfected in weakness." Most gladly, therefore, I will rather boast about my weaknesses, so that the power of Christ may dwell in me. Therefore I am well content with weaknesses, with insults, with distresses, with persecutions, with difficulties, for Christ's sake; for when I am weak, then I am strong. (2 Corinthians 12:7-10 NASB)

Then Jesus came with them to a place called Gethsemane, and said to the disciples, "Sit here while I go and pray over there." And He took with Him Peter and the two sons of Zebedee, and He began to be sorrowful and deeply distressed. Then He said to them, "My soul is exceedingly sorrowful, even to death. Stay here and watch with Me." He went a little farther and fell on His face, and prayed, saying, "O My Father, if it is possible, let this cup pass from Me; nevertheless, not as I will, but as You will." Then He came to the disciples and found them asleep, and said to Peter, "What? Could you not watch with Me one hour? Watch and pray, lest you enter into temptation. The spirit indeed is willing, but the flesh is weak." Again, a second time, He went away and prayed, saying, "O My Father, if this cup cannot pass away from Me unless I drink it, Your will be done." And He came and found them asleep again, for their eyes were heavy. So He left them, went away again, and prayed the third time, saying the same words. (Matthew 26:36-44 NKJV)

You are now enriched with much of the alive and active Word of God's message about prayer. *You are called!* Enlist yourself on God's prayer warrior team!

CRAVE

Challenge: Look up the word "faith" in the four gospels (Matthew, Mark, Luke, and John).

- Document in your SOAR notebook the similarities that you find in every instance where you see the word "faith."

- What did God reveal to you through this exercise? Write it down so that you can *SHARE* later with others.

Read Hebrews 11 and 12:1-3. These verses will give you a boost.

SEEK GOD – Week Eight
Know God through Praise and Worship
SHARE!

Week Seven Review Question: How did Week Seven deepen your understanding of prayer? If you did the Crave section and looked up the word "faith" in all four gospels, what did you find?

Objective: Seeking to know God intimately so that our lives overflow with worship in all that we do!

Memory Verse:

> Exalt the LORD our God and worship at his footstool; He is holy. (Psalm 99:5)

I (Sheri) was at a professional basketball game the other night. As the players ran onto the court, fireworks were going off (yes, inside the building). My kids were mesmerized and entertained! The MC would say, "Scream!" and everyone in the place would get louder and louder. The excitement over this team just making one basket was unbelievable. I saw one man wearing the wildest hat to support his team while others had their faces painted. Whether the basketball team was doing well or not, the fans were sold out! This was *worship*.

Before national championship games, fans prepare for watch parties. They get all the right clothing gear and the right food, and then they explode in cheering and celebration for their team.

I love the Bible verse below, in which it talks about a crowd that gathered to wait for Jesus. They came early—maybe gathering like a parade—and when Jesus, the One and Only, entered, the following took place:

> As soon as He was approaching, near the descent of the Mount of Olives, the whole crowd of the disciples began to praise God joyfully with a loud voice for all the miracles which they had seen, shouting: "BLESSED IS THE KING WHO COMES IN THE NAME OF THE LORD; Peace in heaven and glory in the highest!" Some of the Pharisees in the crowd said to Him, "Teacher, rebuke Your disciples." But Jesus answered, "I tell you, if these become silent, the stones will cry out!" (Luke 19:37-40 NASB)

This is *worship*.

There are two kinds of worship seen in these examples. One is the worship of something that is temporal (basketball) while the other is worship of the Eternal Living God. *What or who do you worship?*

The past seven weeks have been a season to prepare our hearts to worship God. Our prayer is that your life becomes an overflow of worship to the Father. "Whatever you do, work at it with all your heart, as working for the Lord, not for men..." (Colossians 3:23).

GROUP SHARE TIME

During our Share time this week, we are going to worship the Living God.

Everyone has his or her own way to prepare to worship God. Maybe today your life was chaotic, and you didn't have time to settle your heart. Let's take a moment now to do that—through prayer, stillness, or reading a verse. You choose the way that works for you.

If you need a verse, there are many verses in the Psalms that can help you prepare for worship. Pick your favorite, or one of these, and take a few minutes to prepare your heart: Psalm 134, Psalm 63:1-8, or Psalm 150.

Consider this:

- If an investigator looked at your calendar and checkbook, what would he say that you worship?

- For me, he might say that I worship my children. What's your object of worship? Is it your job, service to others, your family, money, health, sports, a hobby, friends, depression, or a negative attitude? Lay it down today. Ask God to give you a heart to worship Him *above* everything else!

- Music is one way to worship. What are some other ways to worship God?

- What are some ways in which you can prepare your heart to worship God?

SEEK GOD – Week Eight
Know God through Praise and Worship
EAT!

Objective: Seeking to know God intimately so that our lives overflow with worship in all that we do!

Memory Verse:

> Exalt the LORD our God and worship at his footstool; He is holy. (Psalm 99:5)

This is our last week. Don't give up—finish the race strong!

Worship. We all do it. Every day our affection, adoration, devotion, honor, and reverence are given to something or someone. Who or what do you worship? All too often my devotion lies with the things of this world. But when we see God for who He really is, worship is true and spontaneous. Our prayer (Amy's and Sheri's) is that the past seven weeks have strengthened your relationship with God in such a way that you are already in an all-out worship mode with the Only One worthy of our worship. In this final week of Seek God, you will study what God's Word says about how we are to worship Him. May you never again be the same!

Day 1   Worshipful Response

Romans 12:1-2 states, "Therefore, I urge you, brothers, in view of God's mercy, to offer your bodies as living sacrifices, holy and pleasing to God-this is your spiritual act of worship." Read 1 Chronicles 29 and look at how worship is a whole-life expression.

In what ways do you respond to God in worship? Meditate on this question. Consider writing down your thoughts in your SOAR notebook.

Day 2   Sincere and Humble Heart

In the following verse, a woman asked Jesus about the right *place* to worship:

> "Our fathers worshiped on this mountain, and you Jews say that in Jerusalem is the place where one ought to worship." Jesus said to her, "Woman, believe Me, the hour is coming when you will neither on this mountain, nor in Jerusalem, worship the

Father. You worship what you do not know; we know what we worship, for salvation is of the Jews. But the hour is coming, and now is, when the true worshipers will worship the Father in spirit and truth; for the Father is seeking such to worship Him. God is Spirit, and those who worship Him must worship in spirit and truth." (John 4:20-24 NKJV)

The following verse from Isaiah gives us an idea of what worshipping "in spirit and truth" looks like:

"When you cry out for help, let your collection [of idols] save you! The wind will carry all of them off; a mere breath will blow them away. But the man who makes me his refuge will inherit the land and possess my holy mountain." And it will be said: "Build up, build up, prepare the road! Remove the obstacles out of the way of my people." For this is what the high and lofty One says—he who lives forever, whose name is holy: "I live in a high and holy place, but also with him who is contrite and lowly in spirit, to revive the spirit of the lowly and to revive the heart of the contrite." (Isaiah 57:13-15)

The words "contrite" and "lowly" are translated from Hebrew words that mean crushed, bruised, broken, and depressed.

When I (Amy) am feeling really down, I like to go to a quiet place and worship God as my hiding place and lover of my soul.

Now let's look at two more passages from Psalms and 1 Samuel.

O Lord, open my lips, and my mouth will declare your praise. You do not delight in sacrifice, or I would bring it; you do not take pleasure in burnt offerings. The sacrifices of God are a broken spirit; a broken and contrite heart, O God, you will not despise. (Psalm 51:15-17)

When they arrived, Samuel saw Eliab and thought, "Surely the LORD's anointed stands here before the LORD." But the LORD said to Samuel, "Do not consider his appearance or his height, for I have rejected him. The LORD does not look at the things man looks at. Man looks at the outward appearance, but the LORD looks at the heart.' (1 Samuel 16:6-7)

True worship comes from a sincere and humble heart. A heart that walks in the truth, obeying God's laws out of love for Him. A heart that has come to the realization that apart from God there is no hope. Worship Him in spirit and in truth.

Day 3   Worship Your Way

Read Psalm 95 through Psalm 100.

Make a list of ways to worship in your SOAR notebook as you read these scriptures. Begin to apply them in your life as a response to *who* God is. He is worthy!

God is not interested in where we worship, or in our cultural style of worship, as long as our worship comes from the love and purity of our spirit that has been reborn in the truth. I (Amy) love to play worship music or the Bible on CD and to worship God throughout my daily activities.

Day 4   Joyful Noise

Read Psalm 148 through Psalm 150.

If you haven't already, it's time to "strike up the band"! God loves for His children to "make a joyful noise" unto Him. Worship Him throughout the day with music, song, dance, shouts, or whatever suits the person whom God made you to be. Rejoice in the God of your salvation!

Our family (Sheri's) worships with music DVDs, dancing, singing, jumping, running, and sometimes just sitting around the table to talk about God. This is worship. How will you worship God today?

Day 5   Worthy of Worship

A friend of Louie Giglio, Bruce Leafblad, defined worship as "centering our mind's attention and our heart's affection on the Lord." Write out your own definition of worship in your SOAR book.

As we conclude our final week of SEEK, let's turn to the last book of the Bible and get a glimpse of worship in our Eternal Home.

Read these passages from the book of Revelation:

> The four living creatures, each having six wings, were full of eyes around and within. And they do not rest day or night, saying: "Holy, holy, holy, Lord God Almighty, Who was and is and is to come!" Whenever the living creatures give glory and honor and thanks to Him who sits on the throne, who lives forever and ever, the twenty-four elders fall down before Him who sits on the throne and worship Him who lives forever and ever, and cast their crowns before the throne, saying: "You are worthy, O Lord, to receive glory and honor and power; For You created all things, And by Your will they exist and were created." (Revelation 4:8-11 NKJV)

And I saw something like a sea of glass mingled with fire, and those who have the victory over the beast, over his image and over his mark and over the number of his name, standing on the sea of glass, having harps of God. They sing the song of Moses, the servant of God, and the song of the Lamb, saying:
"Great and marvelous are Your works, Lord God Almighty!

Just and true are Your ways, O King of the saints! Who shall not fear You, O Lord, and glorify Your name? For You alone are holy. For all nations shall come and worship before You, for Your judgments have been manifested." (Revelations 15:2-4 NKJV)

Now I, John, saw and heard these things. And when I heard and saw, I fell down to worship before the feet of the angel who showed me these things. Then he said to me, "See that you do not do that. For I am your fellow servant, and of your brethren the prophets, and of those who keep the words of this book. Worship God." (Rev 22:8-10 NKJV)

And finally, from Romans:

One man considers one day more sacred than another; another man considers every day alike. Each one should be fully convinced in his own mind. He who regards one day as special, does so to the Lord. He who eats meat, eats to the Lord, for he gives thanks to God; and he who abstains, does so to the Lord and gives thanks to God. For none of us lives to himself alone and none of us dies to himself alone. If we live, we live to the Lord; and if we die, we die to the Lord. So, whether we live or die, we belong to the Lord. For this very reason, Christ died and returned to life so that he might be the Lord of both the dead and the living. You, then, why do you judge your brother? Or why do you look down on your brother? For we will all stand before God's judgment seat. It is written: "As surely as I live," says the Lord, "every knee will bow before me; every tongue will confess to God." (Romans 14:5-11)

Worship God! Hallelujah and glory to the King of kings! Worthy is the Lamb! He is everything!

SEEK GOD
LEAD! Leader Notes

Week One

LEAD! Welcome, leaders! What an awesome journey you are starting. Be encouraged that God will use you, and already is, to train up the body of Christ. We are praying for you! There is an introduction video that we encourage you to share. Prepare an icebreaker; get to know one another; and have fun!

SERVE! This week serve one another. Encourage one another daily and bind up the broken-hearted. Leaders, consider having your group phone each other throughout the week to facilitate this.

LIVE! The first few weeks of meeting together are imperative to developing trust in the group. Consider having a few weeks prior to starting to get to know one another. Another idea is to have a meal together or a strong icebreaker.

Week Two

LEAD! We hope that you are enjoying leading your group through SOAR: Seek God! Be sure to pray for the members of your group. This week the video is short, and we are talking about roadblocks to seeking God. Be prepared to share your own roadblocks. There are many group questions this week. In a larger group size, it might be difficult go through all of the questions. Decide beforehand if you want the group to meet in one large group or in smaller groups, and which questions you want to present to the group.

SERVE! This week share a name or character trait of God with a family member. This is good practice—to give back out what you have taken in. We don't have to have a degree in theology to share with others.

LIVE! Consider having a fellowship to share all the names and character traits of God you have been learning.

Week Three

LEAD! This is one of my favorite weeks. I love knowing God better through His Word. Prepare an activity: As people come into your group, have everyone wear two nametags—one tag for the person's given name and the other for a nickname. This week you are going to search the Scriptures for the character traits and names of God. We have a video (approximately seven minutes) from Craig Groeschel on knowing God. Prepare this week by going through the Scriptures and the character chart so that you will be able to give the participants examples before you start. We used the alphabet to see how many names we could find. You can use this method or whatever method works for you.

SERVE! This week plan a mission trip together for the end of Week Eight so that you can plan to share all that you are learning with someone whom you don't know.

LIVE! Ask your group to engage one another in one-on-one time outside the group.

Week Four

LEAD! Have you ever witnessed a child explore and find new things (things we totally take for granted) with awe and wonder? This week we are going to look at God the Creator with the eyes of a child. We want to encourage you to love your group right where they are and to celebrate every transformation and success!

SERVE! Clean up an area park or something in nature together so that you can continue to see and celebrate God the Creator!

LIVE! Plan a day trip or activity for some outdoor fun.

Week Five

LEAD! This week we embark on a three-week journey to study prayer. We will go through 1) prayer basics, 2) resting and listening to God, and 3) powerful prayers. We have a video from the Prayer series at Lifechurch.tv. It is about 25 minutes long, so plan your time carefully. If you don't watch the video as a group, be sure to watch it in advance so that you can share the basics with your group. We are in Week Five, so encourage real transparency by setting the example. Keep seeking to know God deeply!

SERVE! Pray together on the phone, or pray for others, outside of your group.

LIVE! Grab coffee or dinner, or just do something fun together.

Week Six

LEAD! We hope you are encouraged by how your group is being transformed in this journey. Be sure to keep celebrating together all of the revelation that God is bringing forth. In Romans 1:12, Paul says that they were mutually encouraged. I love this because as leaders, we take such encouragement when the people we are leading truly start to get it. Enjoy the journey! This week, plan for 1) a short video and 2) about 20-40 minutes for individual reflection time, to be still and know that He is God! Consider making places in your home available for private time with the Lord.

SERVE! Hold each other accountable to how well you are maintaining your quiet time. Serve someone this week quietly by praying for them.

LIVE! This week consider having communion together. In an attitude of prayer, together, take the time just to sit and patiently list all of the names and character traits of God.

Week Seven

LEAD! Today, we have the opportunity to pray together. We have a video of Amy and Sheri talking about their prayer journeys. It took us 30 minutes to make this short video. We laughed till we cried. I am sorry if you don't have access to the bloopers! If you prep your group before you start the video, the video will lead you straight into praying with each other. If you don't have a prayer partner, pray and ask God to bring you one. Try to encourage your group members to do so as well.

SERVE! If you know of someone who needs prayer at the hospital, plan to go as a group to pray with this person.

LIVE! Take two weeks to go through the EAT section of Week Seven. In the week where there is no lesson, enjoy each other's fellowship during group time. This is the prime time to assess the progress of your group. For me (Sheri), I ask myself, "Am I gaining altitude with God?" Assess where your group is this week and determine if you want to repeat one or more weeks.

Week Eight

LEAD! This week ... worship! We have a worship DVD for your group. We hope that the hearts of everyone are turning toward worshipping God above everything else in this world. Your group can choose to worship only, worship first, or worship last and still do the Share questions. If you choose not to go through the Share section, we recommend that you encourage your group to read through it at home.

We are wrapping up Seek God this week. Plan a meal together to share all that God is doing. We want you to use all that you are learning and to serve others by praying for them, pouring into someone else that doesn't have these truths, or doing whatever God is calling you to do individually.

SERVE! Worship God with your time. Get your mission trip completed soon. Be sure to share your testimony on how God has changed your life!

LIVE! Worship together with some of the following:

- Read the Bible aloud.
- Read an entry in your SOAR Notebook.
- Sing songs of praise to God.
- Pick something that suits your style of worship.

PART 2

OBTAIN TRUTH

"Then you will know the truth, and the truth will set you free."
(John 8:32)

OBTAIN TRUTH: Outline and Overview

Our study began with Seek God because you cannot receive truth from a God you do not know. The only way that you will trust His word is if you know Him—personally. As you get to know Him through the Bible and spending time communicating with Him in prayer, you will see His character and truly begin to fall in love with your Abba Daddy.

You may recognize that you do not have a relationship with Father God. If you are ready to invite Him into your life, simply pray and ask Jesus Christ to forgive you and inhabit you through the Holy Spirit. If you are not sure of your salvation and you want to be sure, or you do not know what to pray, pray this prayer:

Father, I confess that I have sinned against you. Please forgive me. I ask you to be my Savior. I realize that I could never earn salvation on my own. I fix my trust in Jesus. I believe that Jesus took the punishment for my sin on the cross. I believe that You love me and that Jesus died and rose again so that I can be forgiven and know You. Fill me with Your Holy Spirit. I give You my life. Thank you for loving me and giving me new life. I trust that I am Yours and am now sealed with Your Spirit! In Jesus' name, amen.

You are in Christ! You are His child. Don't doubt it. Do not look back. Walk forward with the Father from now on. Leave your old life of sin and rebellion because you have been made new, clean, and holy!

This study is a perfect way for you to begin to grow in your understanding of what you now have in Christ Jesus and to renew your mind to become more like Him. Welcome to the family of God!

If you want to seek to know Him more, please feel free to go back to the Seek God study; or continue on with us—in Obtain Truth!

Each study builds upon the previous one. Our prayer for each of us throughout this journey is that we will know Him more intimately and that the eyes of our hearts will be flooded with revelation.

Obtain Truth … Today!

"Obtain" is a verb; it implies *action*. So we are going to invest some action into obtaining God's truth and storing it in our hearts. How? Through reading God's Word in daily nourishment portions.

Obtain Truth: Find freedom in God's Word. "Then you will know the truth, and the truth will set you free" (John 8:32).

Study Outline

Week 1: I Need Truth – with Amy (28 min.)

Week 2: I Need Revelation – with Sheri (22 min.)

Week 3: I Am Secure – with Amy (36 min.)

Testimony with Leah Cline

Week 4: I Am Filled with the Holy Spirit – with Sheri (23 min.)

Testimony with Ketric Newell

Week 5: I Am a Priest – with Amy (34 min.)

Week 6: I Am Adopted – with Sheri (28 min.)

Testimony with Dana Byers

Week 7: I Am Loved – with Amy (30 min.)

Skit by Jody Blackwell

Week 8: I Am in a Battle – with Sheri (18 min.)

Testimony with Danae King

Week 9: Transformed by the Truth: REAL Stories of Freedom! (1 hr.)

Week 10: Your Personal Testimonies

Schedule your own testimony share time. Share with others how God has given you revelation, renovated your mind, how you relied on Him and what you resisted. How has God renewed you during this time?

Beloved,

I desire to see the Body of Christ develop a passion and love for the Truth (Jesus, the Word)! Having access to the Bible is an astounding privilege and blessing for believers in Jesus Christ. The Word of God is alive and active! One life-giving verse can change a person forever. It can save, teach, correct, and encourage us. Yet at the same time, it can demolish strongholds and ward off our Enemy. Why would anyone ever want to neglect an amazing gift like this? Why do I ever neglect it? Why would I ever disregard the blessings of being in God's Word?

Too many Christians struggle with knowing how to study the Bible on their own. If they read it at all, they are dependent on a Bible study or a Bible reading plan to help. These are great, but I don't want anyone to have to wait for the next "Bible thing" to dive into the Word again.

The tools in this study can be used for the rest of your life! I often personally use these approaches for my own Bible study time. Exploring the Word on my own, I have gained tremendous insight and intimacy with my Father.

Do you really want to grasp who you are in Christ? Do you long to know all that is yours as His child? Do you want to be set free from insecurities so that you can live powerfully for God's glory? Do you want to go from being spoon-fed to being able to feed yourself? I invite you to come with a spiritual hunger for righteousness.

Teaching and preparing Obtain Truth has been an absolute thrill for me. I pray you will be abundantly blessed by it! "Then you will know the Truth and the Truth will set you free" (John 8:32).

Loving you and Loving Him,

Amy Groeschel

Dear friends,

I raised my hand to receive Christ as a ten-year-old little girl. However, I spent the next sixteen years living as if I had never known Christ. To me, God was an insurance policy that kicked in at my death.

I never had "it!" What is "it"? "It" is a rock-solid relationship with God. I would meet people who seemed have "it." Quite frankly, they freaked me out. I tried to be right with God, but I always fell short and would mentally beat myself up. I never had any peace. I always questioned my salvation.

One day I opened my Bible and started reading it. I loved it! I couldn't believe how much the Old Testament reminded me of my favorite soap opera. As I continued reading God's Word for up to two hours a day, it started to change me—and I didn't even realize it!

On her deathbed, my aunt said, "Either way, I win." "What?" I thought, "I don't know God like she does but I want to!" How was she able to trust God like that? She knew Him and that His promises were true – in life or death! God's Truth is vital! Why, you might ask? Because this world only has death to offer you, but Truth brings life.

I resolved to seek and know God and Truth daily. My prayer is that you will commit to know the Truth with me!

> Now the Lord is the Spirit, and where the Spirit of the Lord is, there is freedom.
> (2 Corinthians 3:17)

Love in Christ,

Sheri

OBTAIN TRUTH – Week One
I Need Truth (with Amy)

Memory Verse:

I keep asking that the God of our Lord Jesus Christ, the glorious Father, may give you the Spirit of wisdom and revelation, so that you may know him better. I pray also that the eyes of your heart may be enlightened in order that you may know the hope to which he has called you, the riches of his glorious inheritance in the saints, and his incomparably great power for us who believe. That power is like the working of his mighty strength, which he exerted in Christ when he raised him from the dead and seated him at his right hand in the heavenly realms. (Ephesians 1:17-20)

Video Review: http://www.soarwithgod.com/Obtain/Obtain.html

"I Need Truth"

- We have a real enemy, the Devil. He doesn't want us to know truth. He is the Father of Lies—the Deceiver.
- Without truth, we are subject to the enemy's STDs:
  - Suppressed Truth
  - Twisted Truth
  - Doubted Truth
  - Sidetracked Truth
- We become vulnerable to sin and lies when the Word is not sharpened within us.
- Unbelief is a lie believed.

Why Knowing Truth is Imperative

Truth	Lies
Frees	Binds (Enslaves)
Guides	Misleads (Sidetracks)
Purifies	Pollutes (Suppresses)
Teaches	Twists (Distorts)
Rebukes	Excuses
Corrects	Blinds
Equips	Distracts (Ineffective/Unproductive)
Generates Certainty	Generates Doubt

Remember this: *"A lie believed as a truth will affect your life as if it were true."*
~ Craig Groeschel

Write down lies that currently deceive people in general. Has God just revealed to you a lie that you believe?

_____

_____

Are you ready to stop being deceived by the enemy? Let's Obtain Truth!

Day 1   Truth is Vital

SEEK GOD

Read and pray aloud Ephesians 1:17-20.

Seek your Father God in prayer. Ask Him for wisdom and revelation to know and understand His truth better. Pray this scripture daily for yourself. It is God's Spirit that opens your eyes to see truths in His Word.

OBTAIN TRUTH

Then you will know the truth, and the truth will set you free. (John 8:32)

All Scripture is God-breathed and is useful for teaching, rebuking, correcting and training in righteousness, so that the man of God may be thoroughly equipped for every good work. (2 Timothy 3:16-17)

Write down in your journal why knowing truth is vital. Express your desires and commitments to knowing God's truth more fully.

Day 2   The Word, Part One

SEEK GOD

Find a quiet place—maybe it's your closet. Lie facedown. Now consider this prayer:

Father, thank You for Your life. Thank You for Your Son. Open my heart to knowing You more intimately. Help me understand the truth through Your Word. In Jesus' name, amen.

The reason we suggest that you get on your face is that in the same way you would bow before a king, you bow before Father God in honor and respect because He is the King of kings.

I never get out of my bed before I hit the ground in prayer to my King. Find your special way to humble yourself before your Holy Father. Adore and worship Him. Christ is your life. Abandon your ways to wholly follow Him. Be still and listen.

OBTAIN TRUTH

Read Psalm 119:1-88.

Today we are going to start reading the longest chapter of the Bible. Read it all the way through or for as long as time will allow.

King David, a man who sought after God's own heart, wrote this Psalm. He uses such words as "ordinances," "commands," "laws," "precepts," "statutes" over and over again. All of these words can be summed up as "the Word"! As you read, I (Amy) want you to substitute these previously mentioned words with "the Word." This will help to bring clarity, and I believe, a greater emphasis and impact to your heart.

Title a journal page "The Word." Write down the truth treasures that you obtain in your reading. You may want to do what I did and make a list of every description of God's Word mentioned. This took me a long time! I had over two pages of notes, but it was totally worth it. If you want to do this or something like it, spend as many days as you need to get the task done.

To me, studying the Word is like studying a painting of a master artist. I love art! The longer I spend looking at a painting, the more familiar I become with the details. I begin to see things that I would have missed if I 'd only looked for a moment. The first chapter of James tells us that the man who looks intently at the Word, not forgetting it but doing what it says, will be blessed! On your mark, get set ... LOOK!

Day 3   The Word, Part Two

SEEK GOD

Read and pray aloud Ephesians 1:17-20. God desires that we love and heed his Word! Respond to God now in prayer. Ask the Father to deepen your love for Him and His Word.

OBTAIN TRUTH

Read Psalm 119:89-176.

How far did you get yesterday? Continue to read and journal "The Word" observations from Psalm 119.

Are you finished with your study of Psalm 119? It's a treasure! Don't take too many shortcuts, or you will miss out.

Day 4   Double-Edged Sword

SEEK GOD

Read and pray aloud Ephesians 1:17-20.

OBTAIN TRUTH

Read Hebrews 4:12 and 2 Timothy 3:16.

Today read Hebrews 4:12 and 2 Timothy 3:16. In your journal, write the title "God's Word." Study today's scriptures and make a list of everything taught about the Bible.

Spend the remainder of your time with God in prayer.

Day 5   Review

OBTAIN TRUTH

Look over your notes from this week. Reviewing your notes will help to reinforce what you are learning, and you may be surprised to discover some new insight that you had previously missed. You may need more time to complete your notes of Psalm 119. This is your opportunity to finish it!

SEEK GOD

Spend the remainder of your time with God in prayer. Review your memory verse.

OBTAIN TRUTH – Week Two
I Need Revelation (with Sheri)

Memory Verse:

> I keep asking that the God of our Lord Jesus Christ, the glorious Father, may give you the Spirit of wisdom and revelation, so that you may know him better. I pray also that the eyes of your heart may be enlightened in order that you may know the hope to which he has called you, the riches of his glorious inheritance in the saints, and his incomparably great power for us who believe. That power is like the working of his mighty strength, which he exerted in Christ when he raised him from the dead and seated him at his right hand in the heavenly realms. (Ephesians 1:17-20)

Video Review: http://www.soarwithgod.com/Obtain/Obtain.html

"I Need Revelation"

1. Revelation (new enlightenment or understanding of truth)

2. Renovate (trash the lies; study and meditate on truth)

3. Rely (rest in and live out of the truth)

4. Resist (resist the devil and stand firm in the truth)

Where are you currently in your discovery of truth? Are you just beginning to understand who you are in Christ? Are you in the process of renewal and renovation? Throw out the junk and replace it with truth. Assess and write down where you are now.

Day 1   Divine Revelation

> *"Most of life's battles are won or lost in the mind."*
>
> — Craig Groeschel, *Soul Detox: Clean Living in a Contaminated World*

SEEK GOD

Seek your Heavenly Father in prayer. Thank Him and ask Him for more understanding. Pray Ephesians 1:17-20 for yourself. It is God's Spirit that opens your eyes to see truths in His Word.

OBTAIN TRUTH

Read Mark 4:1-32.

Ask God for revelation as you read through the text once. Next go back and read it slowly. Take notes on what Jesus taught about the sown Word and the people who heard the Word.

Give yourself time to review the verses that you have studied. Meditation on truth can bring about a deeper understanding. Choose to reflect and meditate on what you are learning.

Day 2   Renovate Your Mind

SEEK GOD

Pray and thank God for His Word and His life. Pray for yourself, quoting Ephesians 1:17-20.

OBTAIN TRUTH

Read Mark 4:21-25, Romans 12:2, and Ephesians 4:20-24.

Today we are going to focus on renovating our minds with God's Word. This reading may require some contemplation. Don't allow resistance or a busy schedule to hinder you. Ask the Holy Spirit for commitment and insight.

Make a new subject heading, "My Role," in your journal. Read today's verses and write down what you learn about a believer's role as an obtainer of truth. Consider reading these verses in various Bible versions on www.youversion.com.

Day 3   Rely on Truth

SEEK GOD

Seek your Heavenly Father, asking Him for more understanding of who He is. Pray for yourself, quoting Ephesians 1:17-20.

OBTAIN TRUTH

Read John 15:1-8 and Isaiah 43:18-19.

Take out your journal page labeled "My Role." Read today's verses and write down what your role is and how you can apply these truths to your daily life through reliance on God. What specifically can you do to stop looking backward and start looking forward, relying on God's Word today?

Day 4   Resist

SEEK GOD

Pray Ephesians 1:17-20 for yourself and your family. God actually wants you to know Him better. Are you getting to know your Father better? Don't give up. The journey has just begun. Tell Father how much you truly want to know Him. Sometimes writing my prayers helps me to love on God without becoming distracted.

OBTAIN TRUTH

Read Mark 4:23-25 (Amplified Bible), Galatians 6:7-10, Proverbs 4:13, 4:23, 7:1-4, and Luke 12:13-21.

After reading, answer these questions in your journal:

- What must you start resisting today?
- What fence do you need to build to protect your renovated mind?

Day 5   Reinforce the Truth

SEEK GOD

Pray to your Father. Worship Him. Thank Him for His Word that is transforming you this week. Ask Him to continue to flood your heart with understanding. Quote Ephesians 1:17-20.

OBTAIN TRUTH

Look over your notes from this week. This will help to reinforce what you are learning. You may be surprised to discover some new insight that God has given you!

Spend the remainder of your time with God in prayer. Thank Him for what He has shown you through the Word. Can you make a list of ten things that He has faithfully shown you? Write your list in an attitude of prayer and thanksgiving.

OBTAIN TRUTH – Week Three
I Am Secure (with Amy)

Memory Verse:

And you also were included in Christ when you heard the word of truth, the gospel of your salvation. Having believed, you were marked in him with a seal, the promised Holy Spirit, who is a deposit guaranteeing our inheritance until the redemption of those who are God's possession-to the praise of his glory. (Ephesians 1:13-14)

Video Review: http://www.soarwithgod.com/Obtain/Obtain.html

"I Am Secure"

- Before we can know *who* we are in Christ, we must know that we *are* in Christ.
- Many doubt their salvation because they still see evidence of the old sin nature. We must know the Word to gain our assurance!
- Believers cannot remain in a sin lifestyle because the Holy Spirit will convict and draw them back to holy living.
- Believers are not instantly sin-free. Becoming like Christ is a process that we must take part in by obeying and abiding in the truth.
- You are saved by grace through faith, not by what you do.
- Jesus paid the debt for all of our sins - past, present and future!

Day 1   Redeemed and Reconciled

SEEK GOD

Pray, quoting Ephesians 1:13-14. Ask God to reveal insight into this scripture. Praise and thank God for what He has and is doing in your life.

OBTAIN TRUTH

Read this question and allow God to set you free with this truth:

How can I be sure that I am really forgiven?

> In Him (Christ) we have redemption through His blood, the forgiveness of our
> trespasses (sins), according to the riches of His grace. (Ephesians 1:7 HCS)

The only way to know truly that you are forgiven is to believe God's Word. God has forgiven you based on what Christ did, not on what you do. Jesus Christ was the perfect God/Man who died so that we might be fully and completely forgiven of all of our sins (past, present and future). Jesus died for the sins of the whole world. Not one sin was left out—except for the sin of rejecting Him.

When you trust in who Christ is and what He did, you receive the forgiveness that His sacrifice provided. Apart from God's full forgiveness, we could not have a relationship with Him and He could not live in us. Everyone in Christ lives in a forgiven state with God, 24/7. The biblical word for this is "justified," which means that God relates to us "just-if-I'd" never sinned.

> And when you were dead in trespasses (sins) and in the uncircumcision of your flesh,
> He made you alive with Him and forgave us all our trespasses (sins). He erased the
> certificate of debt, with its obligations, that was against us and opposed to us, and
> has taken it out of the way by nailing it to the cross. (Colossians 2:13-14)

> He has not dealt with us as our sins deserve or repaid us according to our offenses.
> For as high as the heavens are above the earth so great is His faithful love toward
> those who reverence Him. As far as the east is from the west, so far has He removed
> our transgressions from us. (Psalm 103:10-12)

One reason why we question God's forgiveness is that we believe God has only forgiven our past sins and not our future sins. We mistakenly conclude that any new sins that we commit separate us from God once again.

When we receive Christ into our life, our forgiveness is a settled issue once and for all. The issue now is not forgiveness but understanding how Christ's life within us can set us free from sin's destructive power.

> For if, while we were enemies, we were reconciled to God through the death of His
> Son, then how much more, having been reconciled, will we be saved by His life!
> (Romans 5:10)

So go ahead and receive it! Agree with God and thank Him for His complete forgiveness. This is where freedom begins. You either believe God that you are forgiven, or you are saying that Christ's death on the cross was not sufficient to pay for your sins!

I have swept away your offenses like a cloud; your sins like the morning mist. Return to me for I have redeemed you. (Isaiah 44:22)

Go to Crave at the end of this section if you want a Bible study assignment to do today.

Read your memory verse aloud twice. Read it slowly and believe every word!

Day 2   Forgiven

SEEK GOD

Ask God to reveal to you what being forgiven means. Pray this:

Thank you for sending your son Jesus to die for me. Please reveal to me what it means for me to be forgiven. Thank you. In Jesus' name, amen.

OBTAIN TRUTH

Read this question and allow God to set you free with the truth that follows:

I have confessed my sin; why do I still feel so guilty?

The devil wants you to believe the lie that you are unworthy so that he can keep you enslaved to sin and hopelessness.

We often beat ourselves up about our behavior and our sins. We feel burdened by the guilt and condemnation that we lay upon ourselves! It could be that you are basing your belief about God's forgiveness on your feelings rather than on God's Word. Our emotions can't discern the truth from trash (lies). They only respond to our thoughts. It's dangerous to base truth on how we feel. Feelings come and go, but God's Word never changes.

Make God's Word the final word on what is true about you and your sins. Agree with God each time that you are reminded of your sins, saying something like this: "*Thank you Lord that this sin of _____ was nailed to the cross and that you paid for it completely. Thank you that you have forgiven me and that you'll never hold this sin against me ever again.*"

God's mercy and grace will enable you to turn from the sinful lifestyle that once held you captive. As you believe this more deeply and renovate your mind, you will be set free from self-condemnation. Believe God, believer!

> There is no condemnation for those in Christ Jesus, because the law of the Spirit of Life in Christ has set us free from the law of sin and death. (Romans 8:1)

Please make sure that you understand Romans 8:1. The law of the Spirit of Life has given us grace, mercy, and forgiveness! As a believer in Christ, you are set free! The law of sin and death is a law that simply means, if someone sins then someone must die. Romans 6:23 states, "For the wages of sin is death, but the gift of God is eternal life in Christ Jesus our Lord." Jesus Christ died in our place! He has paid the price for your sin! No guilt, no condemnation, no burden remains! Hallelujah! This is the Good News!

Go to the Crave section if you hunger a Bible study assignment to do today.

Read your memory verse aloud.

Day 3   ABC Study Method

Read 1 John.

SEEK GOD

Ask God to continue flooding your heart with understanding. Ask Him for a deeper love and knowledge of Him.

OBTAIN TRUTH

Read the book of 1 John.

Don't panic! This is a short book. Read it through once without stopping to get a good overview.

To study the Bible, you can use any of various methods. This week we are introducing a new method: the ABC method.

Here is a simple explanation for this study tool:

"A" is for "**A** title" – How would you summarize, in a title form, the passage that you read?

"B" is for "**B**est verse" – What was your favorite verse? There is no right or wrong answer.

"C" is for "**C**alling" – Does this passage call you to a certain task?

The ABC Method will help you to learn from the Word in a new way. Make sure always to understand the context—the circumstances or setting—of the passage in order to attain the meaning more accurately. When you are finished, pray. A Bible study method will not bring revelation—God does! The more important purpose of a Bible study is communion with God. Your relationship with Him is more important than the knowledge you gain.

Read through the memory verse aloud.

Day 4   The Sin of Unbelief

SEEK GOD

Read this week's memory verse again. Ask God to continue to reveal what this scripture means. Consider writing down what is revealed.

OBTAIN TRUTH

Read Deuteronomy 29:10-21 and Hebrews 3:7-19.

After you read through the passage in Deuteronomy, write a brief summary of the key warnings given to the Israelites about their hearts and attitudes. Title a journal page "Warnings/Instructions to Believers."

As you read Hebrews 3, list all of the instructions or warnings given to the believer in Christ Jesus. Pay special attention to the final verse. What was the cause of the Israelites' loss? Why were they unable to enter into God's presence?

You see, grace and faith save, so only rejecting faith (unbelief) in Christ can prevent your salvation. Allow these truths to strengthen your desire to live in a manner worthy of the grace you have received!

Read your memory verse aloud.

Day 5   Under Grace

SEEK GOD

Spend time praying. Ask God for more understanding of what grace means. Ask Him to continue to flood your heart with understanding. Praise Him for what He has been doing in your life.

OBTAIN TRUTH

Read Galatians 3.

Divide a new journal page into two columns entitled "Faith" and "The Law." Read Galatians 3 again slowly and list in your own words the essence of everything taught about faith and the law.

Meditate on the significance of what Paul is teaching here. Rejoice that you are no longer under the Law but, rather, under grace through the precious blood of Christ Jesus! Oh, what a blessed salvation!

CRAVE

Did you finish all five daily nourishment portions? Are you still hungry for more truth? The Crave section gives you additional opportunities to explore the Bible. Consider taking on these challenges.

Read 1 Peter 1, 2 Peter 1:5-15, and James 5:19-20.

Begin a new journal page with the title "The Believer." You know what to do! First read the passage in its entirety. Next write down all that applies to a believer in Christ. This may seem tedious, but remember that we want truth to sink deep and to bring revelation and renovation! We reap what we sow, so this time is well worth your efforts!

Read Hebrews 12.

Here are a few suggestions:

Use the ABC method.

Make a new journal page using the titles "God's Role" and "My Role."

Consider recording questions that you have and asking them at your next group.

OBTAIN TRUTH – Week Four
I Am Filled with the Holy Spirit (with Sheri)

Memory Verse:

> Do you not know that your body is a temple of the Holy Spirit, who is in you,
> whom you have received from God? You are not your own.... (1 Corinthians 6:19)

Video Review: http://www.soarwithgod.com/Obtain/Obtain.html

"I Am Filled with the Holy Spirit"

Did you know that God has deposited the greatest treasure inside of you? It's the Holy Spirit—God's very own Spirit. It's the same Spirit that raised Christ from the dead! The Spirit that lives in you has raising-from-the-dead power! Once you know what you have, you will be forever changed. But first we need to:

- Value Him! The Holy Spirit lives in you.
- Seek Him! You seek what you value.
- Recognize Him! Distinguish the Holy Spirit's voice from your own voice.

Review past times when the Holy Spirit may have prompted you, protected you, convicted you, or drawn you closer to Him.

Day 1   The Counselor

SEEK GOD

Seek your Heavenly Father. Ask Him for a greater understanding of the Holy Spirit who lives in you. He will show you. Continue praying Ephesians 1:17-20 daily. God will give you wisdom and revelation!

OBTAIN TRUTH

Read John 16:5-16 and 2 Corinthians 5:17.

Title a new journal page "What God Gave Me." As you read today's passage, make notes when you find something that God gave you through the Holy Spirit. Don't be concerned with getting this right or wrong. Just try to see these scriptures in a new way. Trust God with the results.

Want to know more about what God gave you through the Holy Spirit? Check out this teaching by our Senior Pastor at Lifechurch.tv, Craig Groeschel:

http://www.lifechurch.tv/message-archive/watch/ghost/1.

Take notes during this message. Compare your notes to your "What God Gave Me" journal page.

Day 2   The Spirit of Truth

SEEK GOD

Seek your Heavenly Father. Ask Him for more understanding of the Holy Spirit in you. Continue praying Ephesians 1:17-20 daily.

OBTAIN TRUTH

Read John 14:15-31.

Today continue with what we started yesterday. Open to your "What God Gave Me" journal page. As you are reading today's passage, add to your list. Take time to contemplate what these things mean to you personally.

Review your memory verse.

Day 3   Receive What God Provides

SEEK GOD

Seek your Heavenly Father. Ask Him for more understanding of the Holy Spirit in you. Continue praying Ephesians 1:17-20 daily.

OBTAIN TRUTH

Read Ephesians 1:13-23.

Incredible news! God didn't leave you helpless or as an orphan! He left you with a seal, guaranteeing your inheritance – guaranteeing your adoption into His family! He left you with power through His Holy Spirit!

Read today's verses. Title a new journal page with two columns, "God's Role" and "My Role." For example, God's role is to give wisdom and enlightenment, while our role is to ask for wisdom and revelation. This might be challenging because you may have to infer what your role is. God's role may seem easy to find or it may not, but we believe this exercise will help you obtain revelation of all that God has given you! Just try it. Ask God to open your heart to see His role and your role.

Want to know more about what God gave you through the Holy Spirit? Watch this video by Pastor Craig Groeschel: http://www.lifechurch.tv/message-archive/watch/ghost/2

Take notes during this message. Compare your notes to your "My Role" and "God's Role" journal page.

Day 4 Gift Giver

SEEK GOD

Seek your Heavenly Father. Ask Him for more understanding of the Holy Spirit in you. Continue praying Ephesians 1:17-20 daily.

OBTAIN TRUTH

Read 1 Corinthians 12, 1 Peter 4:10-11 and John 14:12.

You may have gifts you've yet to discover. Title a journal page, "Gifts available to the believer." Now, consider the spiritual gifts you believe God has given to you and write these down under the title "My Gifts."

Check out this message on all the gifts the Holy Spirit gives! Join Pastor Craig Groeschel now: http://www.lifechurch.tv/message-archive/watch/ghost/3

Look up the verses that Pastor Craig references. If you don't take the time to look them up for yourself, you are less likely to retain them. The essence of Obtain Truth is for each of us to pick up our Bible and do the work it takes to renew our minds.

If you watch the video, revisit the two journal pages from above and add to them. Reread 1 Corinthians 12:31. What should you do with your spiritual gifts?

Day 5   My Body, His Temple

SEEK GOD

Seek your Heavenly Father. Ask Him for more understanding of the Holy Spirit in you. Continue praying Ephesians 1:17-20 daily.

OBTAIN TRUTH

Read 1 Corinthians 6:19 and Acts 19:1-7.

You are filled with the Holy Spirit! I (Sheri) didn't realize this for a season because I didn't readily operate in the fruits of the Spirit (Galatians 5:22-23). We need to be continually filled up with God and His Word in order to see His life (fruit) manifested through us. Title a journal page "The Holy Spirit." Write down everything you learn about the Holy Spirit from these passages and the video below.

Want to know more about the Holy Spirit? Check out this message on being filled with the Holy Spirit from Pastor Craig Groeschel: http://www.lifechurch.tv/message-archive/watch/ghost/4.

Review your memory verse.

CRAVE

Pray. How do you pray best? Face down on the floor? In the shower? Writing out your prayers? On your knees? Find your special way that you communicate best with your Father.

Thank you, Father, for filling me with your Spirit. Thank you that I am not helpless, that I am filled with your power and your Spirit. Thank you that you have given me gifts that I have yet to see and use. Father, continue to open my eyes so that I can truly know all that I have in You. May my life be a vessel that brings You glory. In Jesus' name, amen.

Read the Holy Spirit verses in John 14 and 16. Write down what you learn from each verse.

OBTAIN TRUTH – Week Five
I Am a Priest (with Amy)

Memory Verse:

> You are a chosen people, a royal priesthood, a holy nation, a people belonging to God, that you may declare the praises of him who called you out of darkness into his wonderful light. (1 Peter 2: 9-10)

Video Review: http://www.soarwithgod.com/Obtain/Obtain.html

"I Am a Priest"

When you know who you are, you will know what to do.

- When you know who you are...
  ◦ All believers are priests
- ...you will know what to do.
  ◦ We are called to be like *Jesus*, our High Priest!
  ◦ We are to offer spiritual sacrifices of love by:
    · Serving
    · Giving
    · Fully surrendering our lives

Priestly Benefits:

- God Himself is our inheritance! This world is not our real home!
- Because of our High Priest (Jesus), we have full and confident access to the Throne of God!

Day 1   I Am a Priest of God

SEEK GOD

Thank and praise your Heavenly Father that you are a chosen, holy, and royal priest! Ask to be used for declaring and displaying His glory.

OBTAIN TRUTH

Read 1 Peter 2:4-12.

Seek and ask God for revelation about your identity as a priest. What does this mean to you? Title a journal page "I am a priest of God." Read today's passage. Write down the characteristics of a priest. Remember, all believers are priests. Therefore, when you read through any text about a believer, you can also interject the word "priest," your name, or any other title that identifies a Christian! Recall this every time the Bible speaks about a believer in Christ. See yourself as God's Word declares that you really are!

Today take five minutes to be silent before the Lord. Read your memory verse aloud twice. Remember to read slowly and pay attention to every word. God's Word is living and active!

Day 2   Imitating Jesus

SEEK GOD

Thank and praise your Heavenly Father that you are a chosen, holy and royal priest! Ask to be used for declaring and displaying His glory.

OBTAIN TRUTH

Read John 13:1-17 and Philippians 2:1-18.

Allow God to renovate your mind: "When you know who you are, you will know what to do" (Amy Groeschel).

Let's look at a specific story of who Jesus was and what He did. Because Jesus knew who He was, He knew what to do.

Label a journal page with two columns, "Character of Jesus" and "How I can imitate Jesus." Read today's text. In the "Character" column, write down qualities you see in Jesus' behavior. In the other column, write down how you can imitate Him.

Using an idea from your list, schedule one way to practice imitating Jesus this week.

Day 3   My Priestly Duties

SEEK GOD

Thank and praise your Heavenly Father that you are a chosen, holy, and royal priest! Ask to be used for declaring and displaying His glory.

OBTAIN TRUTH

Read Romans 12.

Write "Priestly Duties" on your next journal page. From Romans 12, list everything that priestly believers (you) are called to do. Try to use your own words as much as possible. This will help you to internalize the Word.

What has God asked you to surrender? Have you surrendered it yet? What is your unique gift for serving the Body of Christ? Are you using it?

Read aloud the memory verse twice. Quietly pray and listen for the Spirit of God's whispers.

Day 4   My Great High Priest

SEEK GOD

Thank and praise your Heavenly Father that you are a chosen, holy, and royal priest! Ask to be used for declaring and displaying His glory.

OBTAIN TRUTH

Read Hebrews 7:11- 28, 8 and 9.

Today's reading assignment may take a while, but it will be worth the effort! Consider breaking this assignment up into two lessons.

Today you are going to get a closer look at your High Priest as you read in Hebrews.

Try using the ABC method described in Week Three to gain insight from these chapters. To refresh your memory, ABC means:

A = A Title
B = Best Verse
C = Calling

When you are finished, review and meditate on the truths you have learned.

Glorify God with a sacrifice of praise! Keep reciting aloud your memory verse.

Day 5   I Am Called and Blessed

SEEK GOD

Thank and praise your God that you are a chosen, holy, and royal priest! Ask Him to make you usable for declaring and displaying His glory.

OBTAIN TRUTH

Read Isaiah 61.

Jesus states in John 20:21, "As the Father has sent me, so I am sending you." Imitator of Jesus (that's you!), are you ready to be blessed? Yes? Okay. First, read Isaiah 61 all the way through without stopping. This is a prophesy given about Jesus Christ, our High Priest, and His chosen people—us!

Take your journal and prepare the title "My Calling and Our Blessings in Christ." As you read through the text a second time, write down each calling and blessing that you have in Christ Jesus.

Praise God! We have an awesome High Priest and an awesome calling! It's time to respond to God with all your heart.

CRAVE

Read Isaiah 58. Try coming up with your own journal heading. See what you can glean from the text about being a priest of God.

OBTAIN TRUTH – Week Six
I Am Adopted (with Sheri)

Memory Verse:

> He predestined us to be adopted as his sons through Jesus Christ, in accordance with his pleasure and will. (Ephesians 1:5)

Video Review: http://www.soarwithgod.com/Obtain/Obtain.html

"I Am Adopted"

- Has your view of God been twisted?
  - Did you only know about God from other people's opinions?
  - God is your Abba Father. He is good and has good intentions toward you.
- God's original design was for you to have His name on your birth certificate, but sin prevented this. Therefore God sent His Son to restore our birthright!
- Terrific news: Through Christ, you have been adopted!
  - You have a new birth certificate.
  - You have birthrights.
  - You have new family responsibilities.

Day 1   Adopted by a Good Father

SEEK GOD

Take a moment to thank God for adopting you into His family. Ask Him for deeper insights.

OBTAIN TRUTH

> *"Put your expectations on God, not on people."*
> — Joyce Meyer

Read James 1:16-18 and Isaiah 43:1-7,16-21.

Today we are going to seek God for revelation about His goodness. I love these verses in Isaiah. When I lost my mom, I clung daily to Isaiah 43:2. I hope you enjoy this precious love letter from your Father, who loves you extravagantly!

Begin a journal page with the heading "A True View of God." As you read these passages, write down who God truly is.

After journaling, sit before the Lord quietly to dwell on one of these verses. Ask God to reveal where your view of Him might be distorted. Ask Him to show you how good He is. Allow any twisted view of God to flee from you and grab hold of the God who loves you passionately. Psalm 86:5 declares, "You are forgiving and good, O Lord, abounding in love to all who call to you."

Day 2   My New Family

SEEK GOD

Thank God for adopting you into His family. Ask Him for more wisdom and understanding.

OBTAIN TRUTH

Read John 1:10-13, Isaiah 44:1-5, Mark 3:31-35, and Romans 8:15-25.

Ephesians 1:5 reads, "He [God] predestined us to be adopted as his sons [and daughters] through Jesus Christ, in accordance with his pleasure and will." Isn't this wonderful news?

You are adopted! In the parent section of your birth certificate, there is a new name: *Abba Father*. Your Abba Father formed you. You were created for His glory. The moment you received Jesus as your Savior, you were immediately plucked out of darkness and placed into the family of God.

You have been restored to your originally designed birth family—the true Israel! In Ephesians 3:5-6, we see Paul explain that all Christians are part of the true Israel. He states, "This mystery is that through the gospel, the Gentiles (non Jews) are heirs together with Israel, members together of one body, and sharers together in the promise in Christ Jesus."

Let's journal. As you read these scriptures, ask God for fresh insight in "My New Family." Use this phrase as your working title. Also ask God to show you what old family bondage you are hanging onto. Adopted child of God, you are not the same. Your old nature no longer has any hold on you. Whoever Jesus sets free is free indeed (John 8:36)!

Today take just five minutes to be silent before the Lord. Read your memory verse aloud twice.

Day 3 My New Birthrights

SEEK GOD

Say this prayer: God, thank you for adopting me into Your family! Father, today I ask for your revelation to know my new family more intimately.

OBTAIN TRUTH

Read Luke 10:17-22, Ephesians 1:19-21, and Revelations 21:1-8.

Your birthright has been restored! Title a journal page "My Birthrights." As you read today's verses, write down the birthrights that have been restored to you. Pray and ask for wisdom and revelation concerning these birthrights.

In Luke 10:19 we read that we have been given "authority" (some Bible versions say "power") to trample the enemy (figuratively speaking, snakes and scorpions). The original Greek word for authority is exousia, *ex-oo-see'-ah*, which means privilege (i.e., force, capacity, competency, freedom; or mastery, delegated influence). We see this same Greek word, as used in other scriptures, translated as "jurisdiction," "liberty," "power," "right," and "strength." Look at verse 19 again and insert these synonymous words in place of "authority." Wow! What an awesome gift we have been given!

James 4:7 instructs, "Submit yourselves, then, to God. Resist the devil, and he will flee from you." This explains how to exercise our authority over the enemy: Submit to God. Resist the devil.

Want to know one more awesome birthright?

Take a look at what Paul wrote to believers in 1 Corinthians 3:21-23: "All things are yours, whether Paul or Apollos or Cephas (apostles of Christ) or the world or life or death or the present or the future-all are yours, and you are of Christ, and Christ is of God." This is so amazing! Child of God, in Christ all things are yours!

If you want still more insight into your birthright, read through all of Romans 8 again.

Read the memory verse aloud twice.

Day 4 Growing Up

SEEK GOD

Be sure to pray before you start today. It's important to understand that God is the One who gives understanding.

OBTAIN TRUTH

Review the memory verse.

Read 1 Corinthians 3:1-3.

Read today's verses. The Father wants you to know Him, rely on Him, and grow up so that He can empower you to bring Him glory on this earth. Don't waste His grace that He poured out for you.

> As God's fellow workers we urge you not to receive God's grace in vain.
> (2 Corinthians 6:1)

It doesn't matter where you are today. What is important is that you draw a line in the sand and say to yourself, "A lukewarm and a non-growing environment is no longer acceptable. I want to mature in Christ, and that begins today!"

Where are you? Circle your answer:

Are you an *infant*, *child*, *teen*, or *adult* in your Christian walk?

Are you on *solid food* yet? Or are you still on *milk*?

How does one grow up? How can you move from milk to solid food?

Ephesians shows us how. Chapters 1-3 are really teaching the milk—the simple Gospel message and who you are in Christ. In chapters 4-6, Paul is showing the believer (you and I) that if our lives look like those of unbelievers, then we cannot possibly be on solid food. He is saying, "Guys, you have to go back and understand who God is and who you really are so that you can get past your selfish desires."

Do you know what happens when you know God and when you know your identity in Him? He sets you free! You begin to love God because of who He is, not because of what He can do for you. You begin to love others because God loves them so much that He sent His Son so that they could have life (John 3:16-17)!

You change. You begin to get white-hot for God because you go from knowing about Him to *knowing Him* intimately!

Finally, there is Ephesians 6:10-24. Now this is what a maturing believer, one who isn't just on milk, can achieve. Such believers are digesting the meat of God's Word. They are able to stand firm in life's battles. They are prepared and victorious!

Are you ready to take your family responsibility seriously? Make a commitment today! Share this decision with your Father God, your small group, friends, and family so that they can be a source of encouragement to you.

Continue reciting your memory verse aloud!

Day 5   A Maturing Family

SEEK GOD

Seek time with God before you begin today. Your relationship with Him is far more important than anything else.

OBTAIN TRUTH

Read Ephesians 4:1-16.

Let's look at some ways to be a maturing family member in God's household.

Make a journal page—you decide how to title the page. Maybe use the ABC method this time. Meditate and seek a deeper understanding from the Word you have studied today.

If you have the time, read through the entire book of Ephesians. Consider journaling on these two topics: "Who God Is" and "Who I am." Read the verses and write down who Scripture says that God is—and what it says about who you are.

Read your memory verse aloud.

CRAVE

Pray to your Father. If you don't know what to pray, try this one:

Father, I don't want to be an infant any more. I want to know Your riches and the authority that You gave me through your Holy Spirit. I want to know You intimately by the name of Abba Father. Father, grant me a spirit of wisdom and revelation so that I can know You more intimately and deeply. Flood the eyes of my heart so that I can know my inheritance, who I am in You and my calling that You prepared in advance for me to do. Reveal to me the power that is in and for me, the same power that You used when You raised Jesus from the dead and seated Him at your right hand. Father, I want to love You better than this. I know that I haven't arrived, but today, at least know I am on that journey!

Read Galatians (yes, the whole book).

You decide how to title your journal pages. Maybe use the ABC method or another title that we used in a previous week.

OBTAIN TRUTH – Week Seven
I Am Loved (with Amy)

Memory Verse:

"Let the beloved of the LORD rest secure in him,.. And the one the LORD loves rests between his shoulders." (Deuteronomy 33:12)

Video Review: http://www.soarwithgod.com/Obtain/Obtain.html

"I Am Loved"

What is your worth to God?

Know this: God loves you so much that while you were still living in your sins, He sent Jesus in exchange for your life (Romans 5:6)!

Believer, you are BELOVED!

Beloved means: dearly loved, adored, esteemed, cherished, prized and valued!

God knows every hair on your head!

- Do you know His love personally?
- Can you see His love in your own life?
- Can you see His love in the Word of God?

Consider His love that He demonstrated on the cross for you!

Day 1   God's Incomparable Love

"The reason we struggle with insecurity is because we compare our behind-the-scenes with everyone else's highlight reel."

— Steven Furtick

SEEK GOD

Pause and ask God for a fresh revelation to know His surpassingly indescribable love for you.

OBTAIN TRUTH

Read Ephesians 3:16-19 and Romans 8:38-39.

Do you ever feel unworthy, unloved, or insecure? It is a massive burden to measure your worth by man's opinion of you and by your own perfect expectations of yourself. Do you sometimes believe that you should just try harder to be "good enough" and that maybe then you will be worth loving? Human love is limited, small, and conditional. Beloved, here is the good news: God's love for you is massive, constant, and eternal! He loved you and chose you even before you were made worthy through His son, Jesus Christ!

Rate your understanding of His love for you on a scale of one to ten:.

1	"I don't know his love."
5	"I know He loves me, but I can't feel it all the time."
10	"I know His love and His presence consistently."

Be honest here because later we are going to look at this again to see if you are gaining understanding and intimacy in God's love for you.

1   2   3   4   5   6   7   8   9   10

We need revelation to grasp the enormity of God's love. Remember, His love surpasses human comprehension! It is supernaturally discerned. We need His revelation to "get it." Title a journal page "I Know God's Love." Describe His love based on what you read as well as on what you hear from God. Please don't rush through this. The reward of gaining this truth is that you will be filled with all of the fullness of God! Freedom awaits.

Today take five minutes to be silent with the Lord. Read your memory verse aloud twice today.

Day 2   Can You See His Love

SEEK GOD

Pause and ask God for a fresh revelation to know His surpassingly indescribable love for you.

OBTAIN TRUTH

Read Psalm 36 and John 3:14-18.

Today we are going to start the process of digging into Scripture to find some attributes of God. An attribute is a quality or trait possessed by someone or something. You will discover that many of God's attributes display His endless love for you!

Title a journal page "Attributes of God" and begin your search through Psalm 36 and John 3:14-18.

When you're finished, go back and draw a heart next to every trait that demonstrates God's love. Get ready for huge blessings as you discover His many deeds rooted in love!

Day 3   God Is Love

SEEK GOD

Pause and ask God for a fresh revelation to know His surpassingly indescribable love for you.

OBTAIN TRUTH

Read Psalm 118.

Fill a journal page with "Who God Is" (His attributes).

God's trademark is love. God is Love. You are the object of His love and affection! Allow your eyes to be opened to see the object of IIis love as you read today's passage.

You will never understand His love for you by looking at yourself. You must look at who He is! We love Him because He first loved us. Marvel at who He is. He is worthy. He has made you worthy through the cross!

Day 4   The Riches of God's Love

SEEK GOD

Ask God for a fresh revelation to know His surpassingly indescribable love for you.

OBTAIN TRUTH

Read Romans 8.

This chapter is powerful! Don't miss out on the treasures in this text. What Jesus Christ did for us is completely due to His mercy and grace. It is because of His love and for His glory that we are His own!

Begin a new journal page with the title "What I have in Jesus." As you read through Romans 8 again, write down in your journal the treasures you discover that you have in Jesus!

Later on today or this week, look over the notes you have taken. Meditate on the truths that God is using to minister to you. Choose to walk in light of who you are!

Continue reciting aloud this week's memory verse.

Day 5   No Greater Love

SEEK GOD

Seek God for a fresh revelation to know His immeasurable love for you.

OBTAIN TRUTH

Read John 19:1-37, John 3:16-17, and Isaiah 52:14.

Begin a journal page with the heading "His Love Revealed on the Cross." Write out everything that Jesus endured because of His love for you. Can you see His love at the cross? God showed you the full extent of His love on the cross! He took the entire burden for you, so there is none left for you to bear! Look intently and carefully at what you read and write. Never allow the story of the cross to become stale from familiarity. It is the most profound act of love known in life. "Greater love has no one than this, that he lay down his life for his friends" (John 15:13).

Rest. Thank God for His intimate love for you. Read your memory verse aloud twice today.

CRAVE

After completing this week's homework, where would you rate your understanding of God's love for you on a scale of one to ten?

1	"I don't know his love."
5	"I know He loves me, but I can't feel it all the time."
10	"I know His love and His presence consistently."

1   2   3   4   5   6   7   8   9   10

Review your journal notes from this week to glean even more understanding about God's love. Also gain a greater insight into His love by taking a journey through your entire journal. Draw a heart by every point in which God reveals His love for you.

Consider posting some of your journal favorites where you could read them regularly.

OBTAIN TRUTH – Week Eight
I Am in a Battle (with Sheri)

Memory Verse:

> This is the victory that has overcome the world, even our faith. Who is it that overcomes the world? Only he who believes that Jesus is the Son of God. (1 John 5:4-5)

Video Review: http://www.soarwithgod.com/Obtain/Obtain.html

"I Am in a Battle"

- There is a battle between your flesh and your spirit.
- The flesh includes your natural or sinful desires, feelings, thoughts, and actions that are void of God's supernatural power and life.
- A giant in the battle: many see themselves as "barely" restored.
- The solution: See yourself as completely restored and new in Christ!
- The way that David won his battle: he knew his God and he knew who he was!

This week we are going to focus on this key component—knowing who you are in Christ.

Day 1   Facing Giants with Faith in God

SEEK GOD

Ask God for the heart and eyes of David so that you can more fully understand your identity in Christ.

OBTAIN TRUTH

Read 1 Samuel 17:1-50.

Today we are going to look at the story of David and Goliath. Some of you heard about this story when you were small and some of you have never heard it. Either way, we are going to look at it through a new lens.

As you read through this powerful story, notice how David faced criticism from his brother, the King, and Goliath yet still had the courage to face the battle in front of him! I am not sure that I would have had the same response. Would you?

David knew so well that he was God's chosen child. He was secure in his Father and his identity—so secure that no one could even shake him right before the battle! This should be our goal as believers. We should know our Father and our identity so well that we run toward our giants with fearless faith as David did (1 Samuel 17:48)!

Divide a journal page in half. On one side, write, "What people thought of David"; and on the other side, write, "What David knew as Truth." You will have to assume a little here. As you read the text, complete your journal columns. Seek to know God and these truths with a David kind of confidence.

Seek God for revelation as you answer the following questions:

- Are you living out of your flesh more than out of the Word?
- Do you believe what others say about you more than what God says?

Read your memory verse aloud.

Day 2   Battle Lessons

SEEK GOD

Ask God for the heart and eyes of David so that you can more fully understand your identity in Christ.

OBTAIN TRUTH

Read Exodus 6 and Daniel 3.

Today we are going to read about two different situations in which God called people. We will see in Exodus 6 that Moses was insecure. He did not know his identity in the Lord. However, in Daniel 3 we'll see three young men who were confident in their Lord to the point of death!

How can we be like the three young men? It is only by knowing God intimately and knowing who we are in Him that we have the supernatural power to win the everyday battles!

Title two journal pages "Lessons from Moses" and "Lessons from Shadrach, Meshach, and Abednego." As you read today's verses, list the lessons you learn from these two stories.

Now title a journal page "Lessons from My Life." Yes, it is your turn! Seek God and evaluate your own life. What have you learned (or failed to learn) about God and who you are in Christ? Consider one event or struggle that brought spiritual insight. In victory or failure, God is faithful to work out all things for your good (Romans 8:28)!

Read your memory verse aloud twice.

Day 3   Knowing God Is Everything

SEEK GOD

Ask God for the heart and eyes of David so that you can more fully understand your identity in Christ.

OBTAIN TRUTH

Read Psalm 23 and 24.

Let's read some of the Psalms that David wrote. They show us how much David loved God and how intimately he knew the Father. Knowing God leads to knowing our identity in Him so that we can stand against our enemies and win the battles between our flesh and spirit!

Title your journal page "My God." Write out everything that describes or demonstrates who God is. If you review slowly enough really to consider these familiar passages, you will discover the richness of God's love for you.

Read through your memory verse aloud.

Day 4   A Heart Like David's

SEEK GOD

Ask God for the heart and eyes of David so that you can more fully understand your identity in Christ.

OBTAIN TRUTH

Read Psalm 27.

In Scripture, David is known as "a man after God's own heart." As God's adopted and holy children, this is how we should all be described!

Today we are going to continue on this journey of investigating David's heart for the Lord and his response to God's love for him. Let's press into the Word even more so that we can obtain a greater revelation about David's security in God, with the goal to live out of the same truths in our lives!

Title a new journal page with these two columns: "God is" and "David's heart." As you read through Psalm 27, write down who God is (his character or attributes) and what you discover regarding David's heart.

Continue reciting your memory verse aloud.

Day 5   My True Identity

SEEK GOD

Ask God for the heart and eyes of David so that you can more fully understand your identity in Christ.

OBTAIN TRUTH

Read Ephesians 1.

David knew who he was, and he was confident in his identity, but we have even a greater covenant with God than David did! We have the Holy Spirit living inside us. David did not. The Holy Spirit fills, guides and teaches us. The Holy Spirit is our deposit guaranteeing our inheritance—our identity! Label a journal page "My identity in Christ." As you read Ephesians 1, list the words and verses that describe your identity in Christ.

Review this list by reading it aloud in front of the mirror daily until you believe it. This may seem a little weird to you, but just give it a try. You will be surprised at the results!

CRAVE

Complete any unfinished reading or journaling from this week's Nourishment sections.

Read Ephesians 2 and 3. As you read, continue adding journal pages with the heading "My Identity in Christ."

Consider keeping a permanent journal of all the battles the Lord has won for you! When David went up against Goliath, he continually remembered how God delivered Him from previous battles.

Choose to remember God's faithfulness. What a glorious and wonderful God we serve!

OBTAIN TRUTH – Week Nine
REAL Stories of Freedom

Memory Verse:

> They overcame him by the blood of the Lamb and by the word of their testimony.... (Revelations 12:11a)

Video Review: http://www.soarwithgod.com/Obtain/Obtain.html

"Transformed by the Truth: REAL Stories of Freedom"

This week at group you watched a wonderful testimonial video. This video included testimonies from several people from all walks of life. They shared their personal stories of how God set them free! We pray that your faith was strengthened from these amazing stories of truth setting these individuals free.

SEEK GOD

Ask God to remind you of something through which He has carried you. Spend some time listening and being still before God. Praise Him for all that He has done for you!

OBTAIN TRUTH

Today title a journal page "My Testimony." What is your story? How has God redeemed your life from the pit? What revelation have you gained from this study that has helped set you free?

This week be sure to share your testimony with a friend or a stranger so that he or she has the opportunity to see the goodness of God!

Also be prepared to share your personal testimony in your small group next week. Maybe your group can make your own "Stories of Freedom" DVD!

PART 3

ABIDE IN SPIRIT

Since we live by the Spirit, let us keep in step with the Spirit.
(Galatians 5:25)

Dear SOAR Participant,

Welcome to the third part of SOAR! Now you will be learning what it means to...

Abide by the Spirit.

What thoughts come to your mind when you read the words "Abide by the Spirit"? What does it mean to "abide" anyway? Why is it important for a believer in Christ? How do you overcome the weaknesses of your flesh and live as Christ? We will explore these questions and more in this section of SOAR: Abide.

Our prayer is that the Holy Spirit will impart life-empowering truth that will deepen your spiritual roots and increase your dependence on Him! Join us as we continue on our SOAR journey.

We love you!

Amy and Sheri

ABIDE:
Outline and Overview

We all want to hear God's voice, but how do you know if it's God's voice or your voice? When you hear Him, how do you respond? What does it look like to follow God on a daily basis? This is what Abide is all about!

Galatians 5:25 reads, "Since we live by the Spirit, let us keep in step with the Spirit." Let's begin Abide and ask God to be our teacher as we go!

SOAR began with Seek God because you cannot receive truth from a God you do not know. Seeking to know God is the foundation of our Christian walk. As you spend time with God in prayer and in the Bible, He reveals Himself and you begin truly to fall in love with your Father.

Maybe you recognize that you do not yet have a relationship with Father God. If you are ready to invite Him into your life, simply pray and ask Jesus Christ to forgive you and inhabit you through the Holy Spirit. Now leave your old life of sin and rebellion because you have been made new, clean, and holy! This study is a perfect way for you to begin to grow in your understanding of what you now have in Christ Jesus and to renew your mind to become more like Him! Welcome to the family of God!

Our prayer for you is that you will know God more intimately, that He will flood the eyes of your heart with revelation, and that you will continually surrender your life to Him, moment by moment!

Study Outline

Week 1: Abiding Death – Spirit-led living vs. ME-led (with Amy)

Week 2: Abiding Faith – Living "as Christ" (with Amy)

Week 3: Abiding Emotions – Surrendering emotions to the control of Spirit (with Sheri)

Week 4: Abiding Power – God's power living in you (with Sheri)

Week 5: Abiding Hope – Keeping hope alive amidst life's trials (with Amy)

Week 6: Abiding Love – The only thing that counts is faith expressed by love (with Amy and Sheri)

ABIDE VIDEOS

Find the videos under the OBTAIN TRUTH tab at www.soarwithgod.com.

ABIDE – Week One
Spirit-Led vs. ME-Led (with Amy)

Memory Verse:

> For we know that our old self was crucified with him so that the body ruled by sin might be done away with, that we should no longer be slaves to sin— because anyone who has died has been set free from sin. (Romans 6:6-7)

Video Review: http://www.soarwithgod.com/Abide/Abide.html

Day 1   Surrender

SEEK GOD

Place your mind, will, emotions, and body under the control of the Spirit. Choose to lay everything down before the Father in authentic, loving prayer.

For example, if you struggle with acting out of your anger, ask God to help you surrender your emotional reactions to Him. If you are making poor choices with your body—maybe immorality, over-eating or substance abuse—confess them to God and ask Him to help you fully surrender.

OBTAIN TRUTH

Take out your SOAR journal and title your first page with the two headings "Old Nature" and "New Nature."

Read Romans 6 and jot down all that you learn about a believer before Christ and a believer in Christ.

Here's an example of what I learned from verses 1 and 2:

Old Nature	New Nature
Sin dominated.	I died to sin.

Now it's your turn to dig into the chapter and gain insight about the old-you verses the new-you in Christ.

ABIDE

Are you living more out of your old nature or the new nature?

Have you drifted from your first love, Jesus, so that now you're the one calling the shots?

Jesus clearly explains in Luke 9:23-24 how a wholly surrendered follower of Christ should live. He declares, "Whoever wants to be my disciple must deny themselves and take up their cross daily and follow me. For whoever wants to save their life will lose it, but whoever loses their life for me will save it.'"

We are called to die to our old nature *daily*! Daily. Actually moment-by-moment would be even more accurate.

This can only be done by relying fully on Jesus and the power of the Holy Spirit in us. The cross we are to carry, I believe, is the cross of dying to ourselves. I don't know about you, but I don't follow anyone very well unless I have given over all self-reliance.

Remember, we are not created new in Christ to be independent and self-sufficient. God wants us dependent on Him. We are called to be slaves to God and His righteousness. Apart from Him, you and I are incapable of anything life-giving. Have you traded a close, vibrant relationship for your own imitation of following Him?

Living from His strength is true freedom! Regardless of your circumstances, He is sufficient to supply your every need.

Respond to God now in prayer.

Day 2   Through the Spirit

SEEK GOD

Draw near to God. He is waiting. Choose to give all your heart, mind, and strength to the Father in authentic, loving prayer.

OBTAIN TRUTH

Speak the memory verse aloud twice.

Before you read, ask the Holy Spirit to be your teacher. Then read Romans 7 and 8:1-17.

Compile a list of "What you have in Christ" from Romans 8:1-17. We could have made this list for you, but then you'd miss out on the powerful discovery process.

Write down in your journal everything God revealed to you through your reading.

ABIDE

Have you ever noticed that Christians still battle the flesh (the old sin-nature)? Unfortunately, this is not always hard to miss. The extraordinary news is that when you died with Christ into the new law of the Spirit, you were given His Life and His Spirit! You were made new, but the old way of life can still creep back in. It shows up in our behaviors and thoughts.

Is there a sinful behavior in which you are still participating or that you have given up on overcoming? Are you ready to surrender this to God?

Ephesians 4:22 states, "Get rid of, throw off, put to death, do away with your old life, nature, or flesh." Why? Because we are new creations! Your former life is rotten, dead, and stinky. It doesn't belong to you anymore. So, keep it out of your new life and follow Jesus wholeheartedly.

Through the Holy Spirit, we have access to God's nature and His power to overcome our flesh. You and I can diligently try our best to "be good" in our own power. We will fail every time with self-effort. But we ... you ... can always overcome through the Spirit (Romans 8:13). Always.

When I was seven, I accepted Christ as my Savior. I clearly remember my new nature (the Holy Spirit) changing me. My desires and thoughts were different. I suddenly *wanted* to please God and not my selfishness. I began to hate sin and love people. I was a witnessing machine! I shared Christ at the bus stop, in my home, on the phone, at recess, wherever I lost people were. Not because I had to. I wanted to. I cared so much.

Through my teen years, I had tremendous struggles because I began to follow the ungodly lifestyle of my peers. Peer acceptance became more important than my Father's. Over the course of two years, God's Spirit gently and lovingly drew me back to Him. On November 19, 1989, my prodigal heart came home. I was brought to repentance through my own misery and God's kind conviction.

Since that November, I have yearned to follow the Spirit more and more, wholeheartedly. God is still on the job of refining and perfecting me. I am so thankful for His patience, aren't you?

God is amazingly faithful! The Holy Spirit will complete in you what He began. Let Him have all.

Write or say a prayer to your Heavenly Father. Allow your heart to respond to Him with questions, surrender, praise, and requests.

Day 3   Kick Sin Out

SEEK GOD

Nothing will be able to separate you from the love of God. He will never leave you nor forsake you (Romans 8:38-39). Pause and meditate on these promises and give thanks to God in prayer.

OBTAIN TRUTH

Recite the memory verse aloud.

Read Ephesians 4:17-32 and 5:1-21.

In your journal, write down two headings: "Take Off" and "Put On." Under each heading, identify what you are called to do as a follower of Jesus Christ.

Process the answers on your list. What do you need to take off? Put on? Pray and ask God to help you be transformed in this process.

ABIDE

I recently read this comment on YouVersion.com about the *old self*:

> Very easy to let my old frame of mind, when I was living for myself, creep up and start controlling my decisions. Important to remember there is a conscious choice ... to keep the new self refreshed and full of life by staying submerged in God's word.

I can relate to this person's statement. Can you? My old nature is not always willing to lie down and die. At times it wants to get up and throw a humongous party. How can our new nature overcome this menacing adversary?

Here are two practical ways:

1. Be engaged in the Word of God, meditating on the truth.

2. Choose continuously to "put on" joyful obedience.

Let me simply clarify: Joyfully know and obey the Word!

> *"Faith requires following the power of a whisper."*
> — Shannon L. Alder

As we seek to live righteously, our aim should be to know the Righteous One (God) more and more. He is our righteousness! As we deepen our relationship with God, we love Him more. Love wants to please and submit to the object of its affection. We were created anew to live with God in true righteousness and holiness. Walking with and for the Father is not a chore but rather the most satisfying, peaceful, life-giving thing that we will ever do.

Do you need to turn from some sin that has stolen its way back into your life? Let me help identify some of the ugly suckers (yes, suckers, because sin is a parasite, stealing from your life!): greed (which is idolatry and stems from ungratefulness), rudeness, gossip, rage, self-righteousness, envy, selfishness, addiction to something other than God, pride, vanity, unbelief ... Okay, was that enough to get you thinking?

Maybe you've tolerated a certain sin because you've wrongly believed, "This will never change in me." This is a lie. Don't ever give up. Get rid of it. Disobedience to God causes you to be spiritually dull. Get alert, sharp, and on fire! Simply confess the sin to God and turn away (or maybe run away) from it. You will overcome your flesh and your spiritual enemy when you choose God's path.

Day 4   It's Not My Life

SEEK GOD

Seeking God should be a blessed time of true intimacy. Never rush friendship with the King of kings! This King is our amazing Father! He is the Father of fathers! Give Him your fullest attention right now in relationship.

OBTAIN TRUTH

Say the memory verse aloud to help you remember it: "For we know that our old self was crucified with him so that the body ruled by sin might be done away with, that we should no longer be slaves to sin— because anyone who has died has been set free from sin" (Romans 6:6-7).

Read Galatians 5:16-26 and Colossians 3:1-14. On a new journal page, create two columns, "Death" and "Life." From these verses, write down those things that bring death or bring life.

ABIDE

We already have all of the Holy Spirit, but becoming like Him and producing His fruit is a process. This transformational journey is known as sanctification. At salvation, Christ calls you to lay aside all that is not of the Spirit and to give Him control of every area of your life.

You have learned this week that you have a part to play as to which nature comes from your life. You have an ongoing choice. Living the abiding life is achieved by your continuous choice to surrender to God.

If we believe and trust God and His Word, we should imagine, speak, and live from that faith. We should obey Him. Basically, we should choose life.

To obey means to adhere to, abide by, act in accordance with, conform to, follow, and stick to. Obedience also means to do what someone says, carry out someone's orders, submit to, defer to, bow to, yield to, give in to. We must allow Christ, in whom we are hidden, to have His way in us.

If this is not your reality, then ask God to increase your faith as you seek Him. We are all vulnerable to sinful desires that allow our minds to be swept up in worldliness and ungodliness when our faith is weak.

Revolutionize your thoughts and your life with this truth: Christ is your life (Colossians 3:4)! Let me explain this truth with an example from my life.

Just yesterday I was tempted not to return a phone call that I promised I would make. To call would mean that I would be placing myself in an uncomfortable situation. My flesh did not want to do it. I wanted to forget about doing what was right! (Oh, how I love comfort!) However, my new nature knew that it's always best to obey and please God rather than my selfish desires. So I chose obedience to God and death to my unloving, selfish old flesh and made the call.

Okay, so ... the annoying circumstances that I had anticipated still occurred. But I had peace, genuine love, and patience that were truly otherworldly.

As you choose to abandon your way for God's Way, something supernatural happens in you. You become like Christ Jesus!

Choose to walk in the reality of who you really are!

Day 5   Dress Your Best

SEEK GOD

Quiet your mind and take a deep breath. Fully give your whole being (your mind, will, emotions, and bodily strength) to the control of the Holy Spirit. Choose to lay everything down before the Father in authentic, loving prayer.

OBTAIN TRUTH

Say the memory verse aloud.

This week we have been learning how to live a life that dies to our flesh. I have been intentionally redundant in hopes that the truth of abiding in death to self would sink in. Today we will look at what is needed to be prepared fully in all of life's battles.

Go to Ephesians 6:10 in your Bible. Open your journal and jot down the topic "The Armor of God." As you read through Ephesians 6:10-18, compile a list of what the armor is and what it is used for. Keep in mind that the armor is symbolic of what we have in Christ.

ABIDE

Our struggle is not really with people, is it? People are never truly the enemy. We are in an ongoing spiritual battle. The Bible teaches us to use the "armor" for our strength, protection, and preparation in good works. We have been equipped for spiritual warfare!

God gave us His truth, His righteousness, His Gospel, His faith, His salvation and His Word. The armor is His and, essentially, the armor is Him! The command given is: "Be strong! Stand firm! Then, after having done that, STAND!" Stand "in the Lord", in His might and power, and in His armor!

You cannot successfully manage life's battles in your own strength. It is only through the risen Savior, Jesus, that you can overcome Satan's attacks. When you know God, you're certain you can place all your trust in Him. Faith in Him creates the ability to stand firm because you know He is trustworthy, mighty, and lovingly faithful. You know that He will never leave you or forsake you. Dress your best. Clothe yourself with Christ. Continue in your pursuit to know the Father more and more. He is your Source, period.

Here's one more thought to keep in mind:

> So, if you think you are standing firm, be careful that you don't fall! No temptation has overtaken you except what is common to mankind. And God is faithful; he will not let you be tempted beyond what you can bear. But when you are tempted, he will also provide a way out so that you can endure it. (1 Corinthians 10:12-13)

> *"If the Lord fails me at this time, it will be the first time."*
> — George Mueller

This verse is crucial for our understanding of how to defeat temptation.

Are there any temptations in your life right now? Take a moment to list them and offer them to God. Ask Him to show you the way out from under them.

_____

_____

_____

_____

We can be sure that all temptation, no matter how great, has an escape route. We must choose to escape. Choose not to say that unkind word. Choose not to control by manipulation. Choose the blessing of obedience and make a break for the exit door.

Remember, we must not be too confident in ourselves to consider ourselves above falling into sin. Remain humble and dependent on God's strength.

CRAVE

Read James 1:13-27.

There are various methods that can be used to study Scripture. This week we are introducing a new method—the ABC method. If you went through the second part of SOAR, Obtain Truth, then you'll remember the ABC study method.

Here is a simple explanation for this study tool:

"A" is for "**A** title" – How would you summarize, in a title form, the passage that you read?

"B" is for "**B**est verse" – What was your favorite verse? There is no right or wrong answer.

"C" is for "**C**alling" – Does this passage call you to live out a certain task?

The ABC method will help you learn from the truth in a new way, but a Bible study method will not bring revelation—God does! The more important purpose of a Bible study is communion with God. Your relationship with Him is more important than the knowledge you gain.

ABIDE – Week Two
Living "as Christ" (with Amy)

Memory Verse:

> I have been crucified with Christ and I no longer live, but Christ lives in me. The life I now live in the body, I live by faith in the Son of God, who loved me and gave himself for me. (Galatians 2:20)

Video Review: http://www.soarwithgod.com/Abide/Abide.html

> The life I live in the body, I live by faith in the Son of God. (Galatians 2:20)

The life I live, I live by _____.

To *abide* is to live by _____ in Jesus.

Abiding by faith is "_____" with the Spirit. Since we live by the Spirit, let us keep in step with the Spirit (Galatians 5:26).

> Trust in the Lord with all your heart and lean not on your own understanding; in all your ways acknowledge him, and he will make your paths straight. Do not be wise in your own eyes; fear the Lord and shun evil. (Proverbs 3:5-7)

You don't live by faith all on your own!

> For God is working in you, giving you the desire and the power to do what pleases him. (Philippians 2:13)

> To this end I labor, struggling with all his energy, which so powerfully works in me. (Colossians 1:29)

Jesus is our best example of an Abiding Life: "...I love the Father and I do exactly what my Father has commanded me" (John 14:31).

Day 1   Live by the Daddy

SEEK GOD

Draw near to God in prayer, your heart filled with a confident and patient hope. Enjoy the richness of His fellowship.

OBTAIN TRUTH

Recite this week's memory verse aloud.

What does it truly mean to abide?

John 15 gives an excellent picture of the abiding life through the example of a tree. Read the words of Jesus in John 15:1-8. We will read more from John 15 later in our study. Journal a list: "How do I live by my Daddy?"

ABIDE

To remain or abide in Jesus, the Vine, is to live by faith in Him. The Vine is the source of good fruit. Galatians 5:22-23 explains what the fruit of the Spirit looks like: love, joy, peace, patience, kindness, goodness, faithfulness, gentleness, and self-control.

The fruit of the Spirit lives in you at salvation because the "fruit" is the nature of God. His nature or fruit is manifested through you when you abide in Him. You see, it's not about your effort to love and produce joy. A thriving relationship with the Living Vine is what produces His fruit in your life!

Notice I said, "a *thriving* relationship." Good fruit comes from a healthy plant. To be spiritually healthy, God, the Gardener, needs to water your faith with the Word and prune your flesh. You need to trust and depend on Christ to carry out His work in you. Please understand, though, that the simplicity of abiding does not mean it is effortless. You must cooperate with God's pruning and allow God to shine His holy light continually on your heart.

Read the list below and circle the areas in which you need to "let go and let God."

LET GO	LET GOD
My way	His Way
My doubt	His Truth
My strength	His Power
My understanding	His Wisdom
My fear	His Peace

My pride	His Humility
My anger	His Kindness
My independence	His Calling
My selfishness	His Love

Take your circled areas of weakness to God in prayer. Believe in His power to change and heal you.

Day 2   Come to Me

SEEK GOD

Choose to surrender yourself completely to God. Pray your memory verse aloud two times. Pour out your heart to God in prayer.

OBTAIN TRUTH

Today's reading assignment is printed out for you. Read the words of Jesus slowly to take in its entire meaningful flavor. Read it again and again until you are ready to respond to God with a written prayer in your journal.

> "Come to me, all you who are weary and burdened, and I will give you rest. Take my yoke upon you and learn from me, for I am gentle and humble in heart, and you will find rest for your souls. For my yoke is easy and my burden is light." (Matthew 11:28-30)

ABIDE

I have realized that whenever I become familiar with something, like driving the same route home, I mentally check out and go into autopilot. I rely on my routine, my habit, and my abilities to get me through. Friends, this is not how God intends for His children to live.

The other day I drove right past my turn to get to the dentist. I was unconsciously taking my common, weekly route that brings me to my girl's dance lessons. It's no shock that I could make such a mistake since I typically only go to the dentist twice a year.

Let's look at the spiritual lesson here. We form habits of relying on our own experiences, knowledge, and abilities rather than staying fully alert to the promptings of the Holy Spirit. We even tend to do this while reading familiar passages in the Bible.

Take a fresh look at two passages that are paraphrased beautifully in The Message Bible:

"Are you tired? Worn out? Burned out on religion? Come to me. Get away with me and you'll recover your life. I'll show you how to take a real rest. Walk with me and work with me-watch how I do it. Learn the unforced rhythms of grace. I won't lay anything heavy or ill-fitting on you. Keep company with me and you'll learn to live freely and lightly." (Matthew 11:28-30 MSG)

Trust God from the bottom of your heart; don't try to figure out everything on your own. Listen for God's voice in everything you do, everywhere you go; he's the one who will keep you on track. Don't assume that you know it all. Run to God! Run from evil! (Proverbs 3:5-7 MSG)

What about you? Do you rely on your own understanding or past experiences to get you through the day? Are you willing to do whatever is necessary to become spiritually awakened to the reality that Christ is to *be* your life? If so, what will you need to change in your daily routine in order to follow the Holy Spirit more completely?

_____

_____

_____

Acknowledge God as your guide, your ever-present help, your rest, your strength, and everything you need!

Day 3   To Know You More

SEEK GOD

Pray your memory verse aloud. Ask God to lead your every thought and step. Quiet your heart before God in prayer. Listen for Him.

OBTAIN TRUTH

Read John 14:5-14.

Title your journal page "Jesus." Assemble a list of everything that Jesus says about Himself and His "faith-full" followers.

The disciples spent time with Jesus in the flesh. They walked with Him and were eyewitnesses to many miracles, yet Jesus said to them in John 14:9, "Don't you know me?" Abiding in Christ is a continuous journey of knowing Him more and more intimately. The longer you know God, the more you are conformed to His image.

ABIDE

Verses 13 and 14 are powerful statements:

> "And I will do whatever you ask in my name, so that the Father may be glorified in the Son. You may ask me for anything in my name, and I will do it." (John 14:13-14)

"Whatever" we ask? Ask "anything?" What an amazing promise! Notice the phrases "in my name" and "that the Father may be glorified." These words readily define genuine abiding. The emphasis is on our relationship with Christ and glorifying God.

1 Corinthians 2:16 proclaims that "we have the mind of Christ."

Living with the mind of Christ means that your desires are *His* desires and, therefore, you can pray and live according to *His* will and for *His* glory. Trust God when your requests are not delivered as you thought they would be. Continue to do your part and abide. Create a habit of dwelling on God and His truth. Remember, Romans 8 teaches that the mind controlled by the Spirit is life and peace! The longer you walk with God the greater your faith will grow and strengthen because you've experienced His faithfulness.

Spend the remainder of your time in devoted prayer with your Father. Pursue knowing Him. Saturate your emotions, thoughts, and bodily energies in Him.

Day 4   I Will Follow You

SEEK GOD

Pray over this week's memory verse. Acknowledge that your life is not your own. Pursue Christ Jesus, who is your life. Place all of your attention on loving, trusting, and obeying Him.

OBTAIN TRUTH

Your Scripture reading is printed below for you today so that you can focus on the words of Jesus. Circle, highlight, or underline anything that stands out to you regarding how Jesus *abides in* the Father.

But first allow me to give you the setting of today's text. Jesus was healing on the Sabbath and calling God His own Father. Because the Jews measured their righteousness by how well they followed the law, many Jews were questioning and persecuting Jesus for His actions.

Jesus responded with this answer:

> "Very truly I tell you, the Son can do nothing by himself; he can do only what he sees his Father doing, because whatever the Father does the Son also does. For the Father loves the Son and shows him all he does. Yes, and he will show him even greater works than these, so that you will be amazed." (John 5:19-20)

> And then in John 5:30, Jesus says, "By myself I can do nothing; I judge only as I hear, and my judgment is just, for I seek not to please myself but him who sent me.'"

And now, in John 16, Jesus explains a function of the Spirit of Truth (the Holy Spirit):

> "When the Spirit of truth comes, he will guide you into all truth. He will not speak on his own but will tell you what he has heard. He will tell you about the future. He will bring me glory by telling you whatever he receives from me. All that belongs to the Father is mine; this is why I said, 'The Spirit will tell you whatever he receives from me.'" (John 16:13-15)

We are called to become like Christ! Write the title "WDJD" (What did Jesus do?) on a new journal page. Based on the text from John 5, record Jesus' explanations of how He lived.

ABIDE

Now it's your turn to consider the following questions:

- What do I do?
- If Jesus only did what the Father did, how should I live?
- Am I asking for God's direction?
- Have I learned how to listen to and discern God's voice?

Be honest. Have you been living out of total dependency on God or from self-reliance? Maybe you've never believed that it was possible to live how Jesus lived. The truth is, not only is it possible but it is also how we are called to live!

Begin today, asking God for His assignments rather than asking Him to bless your own agendas. Start the morning by asking the Father, "*What would you have me do today? Father, interrupt my plans. Please give me ears to hear and eyes to see you.*"

Before you write an email, make a phone call, or have a conversation, ask God about what to say and how to say it. God is waiting for you to give Him full reign over every detail in your life. He really is. And He is a detail genius!

The song Trent Austin sang for us, "Where You Go, I'll Go" by Brian and Jenn Johnson, proclaims it all: "How could I expect to walk without you when every move that Jesus made was in surrender?"

Oh to truly understand your unity with Jesus, to clothe yourselves with Him and walk as He walked! It's time to stop living life outside of God's strength and guidance. Surrender all. Depend fully. God wants you to abandon everything to Him and have complete control of your life. He needs you to remain tuned in and listening. All of Hell desires that you remain in a state of spiritual apathy and self-dependence. I'd suggest that you and I say, "Hell, NO! No sin or distraction will stop me from doing God's will!"

Spend the remainder of your time visiting with the Father in prayer. Ask Him to reveal anything that is holding you back from full dependency on Him.

Day 5   Listening

SEEK GOD

Pray your memory verse aloud. You are God's treasured possession and true delight! Give your whole mind, heart, and strength to loving your Father in prayer.

OBTAIN TRUTH

Read John 10:1-18.

Write these three titles on a journal page: "The Shepherd/Gate," "The Thief," and "The Sheep." Record all that you learn about each group.

ABIDE

Hearing from God is essential for all believers. Yet many of us are unsure of how to hear God's voice. We vacillate, thinking, "Is this God's voice, my voice, or the thief's voice? How do I know? What does His guidance actually sound like?"

Have you ever tried to hold a conversation with a friend amongst a crowd of people? It's hard to do! It's difficult to communicate with the various distractions and noises that demand our attention.

Be assured, God is trying to communicate. Turn off the radio in your car, the television or computer at home, and even, yes, even your cell phone. Give yourself the gift of silence and wait on the quiet voice of the Spirit. Psalm 46:10 says, "Be still, and know that I am God...." Learn the habit of being still (quieting your soul) and listening for His guidance.

Don't get worried or upset if it seems that God's voice is silent. In the Psalms we see the esteemed King David, who was regarded as "a man after God's own heart," often lamenting wearily as he waited for God to speak and reveal His presence.

Expect God to speak through the Bible, His people, and sometimes even circumstances. He also will speak through whispers, in which His voice speaks quietly to our hearts. These whispers may sound like your own thoughts, except that they are usually uniquely different in content—but they are His voice. You will be less distracted and hear Him clearly if you are tuned in and abiding with the Spirit.

I encourage you to ask God to help you be sensitive to His voice and to liveLL in constant communication with Him. Friends talk to friends, and friends listen to friends. You are a friend of God! And what a wonderful friend you have in Jesus!

ABIDE – Week Three
Surrendering Emotions (with Sheri)

Memory Verse:

> You keep him in perfect peace whose mind is stayed on you, because he trusts in you. (Isaiah 26:3 ESV)

Video Review: http://www.soarwithgod.com/Abide/Abide.html

> For where you have envy and selfish ambition, there you find disorder and every evil practice. (James 3:16)

What has living out of your emotions cost you?_____

CHOOSE to A.B.I.D.E.

A_____ with God.

God won't force you to agree with Him. (1 Corinthians 13)

"The tongue has the power of life and death...." (Proverbs 18:21)

B_____ His Word.

"'The Spirit gives life; the flesh counts for nothing. The words I have spoken to you—they are full of the Spirit and life.'" (John 6:63)

"Do not conform to the pattern of this world, but be transformed by the renewing of your mind. Then you will be able to test and approve what God's will is—his good, pleasing and perfect will." (Romans 12:2)

I_____ triggers.

"'Peace I leave with you; my peace I give you. I do not give to you as the world gives. Do not let your hearts be troubled and do not be afraid.'" (John 14:27)

D_____ your body.

"No, I strike a blow to my body and make it my slave...." (1 Corinthians 9:27)

E_____ yourself.

...but David encouraged himself in the LORD his God. (1 Samuel 30:6)

You will make known to me the path of life; In Your presence is fullness of joy; In Your right hand there are pleasures forever. (Psalm 16:11)

You can learn more from Scripture passages about David (1 Samuel 30), Moses (Numbers 20), and Cain (Genesis 4).

Day 1   Stop the "Emotion Commotion"

SEEK GOD

Identify which triggers cause your dashboard warning lights (the example from this week's message) to flash. Ask God to reveal to you where you are abiding by your emotions rather than by the Holy Spirit.

OBTAIN TRUTH

Read this week's memory verse aloud.

Currently are you living more out of your mind, will, and emotions than by the truth of God's word? How do you know?

A thought leads to an emotion, and the emotion leads to an action. In my (Sheri's) case, a thought can lead to an emotion, then a more negative thought, a stronger emotion, another negative thought, and, finally, an action! It is what I like to call a nasty train-wreck – an "emotion commotion"!

It can mentally and emotionally eat me up ... if I allow it to do so! However, thoughts and emotions can only control you if you cooperate with them.

I have learned that I have certain triggers that cause me to ride on this emotional train. We will talk more about triggers later.

Read Galatians 5:19-20. These are the acts of the sinful nature. Each of these acts has a natural emotional response. Brainstorm in your journal: Which emotions generally result from these acts of your flesh? For example, impurity can result in the emotions of loneliness, sadness, and unworthiness.

Identify your negative emotions. Now ask God to help you know which act of your flesh might be causing or triggering that emotion.

Read the remainder of Galatians 5 and write down the answer to this question: "What are the thoughts or feelings you should experience when you are abiding in the Spirit of God?" In what ways have you experienced or seen the Spirit manifest His fruit in you?

ABIDE

How can the Spirit control your thoughts and emotions? Galatians 5:24 specifically explains that we have crucified the sinful nature with its passions and desires.

When we engage that old self—our old, sinful nature—we get stinkin' thinkin' and "emotion commotion." Some refer to this as "drama." You know what I am talking about.

This subject on emotion runs deep. It will require prayer and much meditation. Write down all that God reveals to you over the week.

Let me encourage you with some of my struggles.

I use to be consumed with worry. I worried about everything – war, terrorist attacks, death, sickness, poverty, rain, being rejected by a friend, finding a mate, work, etc. If you could worry about it, I did! I was always dwelling on what-ifs and the worst-case scenario.

Not any more! Worry no longer dominates my thoughts. How did I overcome worry? I did some practical things. But it started with knowing God. 1 John 4:18 says, "...There is no fear in love. But perfect love drives out fear, because fear has to do with punishment. The one who fears is not made perfect in love." The more I got to know God and His amazing love for me, the more I gained greater freedom from worry.

I did other things, too. You'll find out about them as we go through the next few days. Here is a summary of some of the things I do to emotionally *ABIDE*:

- **A**gree with what God says is true.
- **B**elieve God's Word over my or others opinions.
- **I**dentify triggers that cause negative thoughts.
- **D**eny the flesh through fasting and exercise.
- **E**ncourage myself in the Lord with truth.

I still fall short, but I have so much more victory than I once did.

You need to understand that the old sinful nature was crucified with Christ but your flesh, old thought patterns, and habits may still rise up in you. Yet they have no more authority over you! Emotions are powerful, but you can choose to walk in this truth rather than in emotions that come out of your flesh. Take captive every thought and emotion in your soul that sets itself above the truth. (2 Corinthians 10:5)

Write a list of 100 things that bring you joy throughout this week. At the end of the week, see how it changed your perspective.

Day 2   Triggers

SEEK GOD

Continue to ask God to reveal triggers that cause you to operate out of the flesh rather than out of the Spirit.

OBTAIN TRUTH

Some of my (Sheri's) adverse emotional triggers include being overly hungry, excessively tired, and seeing my home become a cluttered mess. I am more likely to strike out at my husband or children when I am hungry. My family says I turn into military mom if our home is extremely disorganized! They join forces to protect one another.

I don't want to be known as this terrible person I can become in my flesh. It's purely selfish! I am putting my needs and desires above everyone else in these situations. This makes me nothing short of an adult brat!

What about you? Do you know your triggers yet? If you don't, just ask someone who knows you well.

Read 2 Samuel 11:1-5, Numbers 20:7-12, and Genesis 4:3-8. Title a journal page "Triggers of David, Moses and Cain." Title another page "My Triggers" for use later.

What were David's triggers? What was Moses' trigger? What was Cain's trigger?

Write down, on the page labeled "My Triggers," the personal trigger areas that God reveals to you. Keep this page handy throughout the week. Be aware of when you act out of the flesh and write down what you believe was the root cause.

ABIDE

Emotions are helpful tools when we know how to use them.

When my first child was a baby, she had a fever of 105. I was so scared! I took her to the doctor and he told me this: "It's a virus. It will run its course. Don't panic. But…" he hesitated before saying, "I am sure you are not going to like this: If you can stand it, let her run the fever. The fever isn't the problem. It's just an indictor that there is a problem. The heat of the fever can kill the virus."

I wondered about that all day. The fever isn't the problem? It's just an indictor that there is a problem?

Just like fever is an indictor of a problem, so are our emotions. Emotions are indicators, but we often misuse them.

Emotions are helpful tools *if* we know how to use them. Remember the dashboard warning lights? Imagine if, when you saw the warning lights, you punched the passenger instead of opening up the hood of the car or praying? That would be foolish!

Yet that is basically how we react in our flesh! Something triggers our thoughts and emotions, and we respond by striking out and hurting someone or by withdrawing from God rather than looking for the reason behind the trigger! That is sad. The poor emotional response is warning us of an internal condition in our heart.

We, the body of Christ, should not misuse emotions, which God has given us, to the harm of others. Instead we need to use them to identify what is causing us to step away from intimacy with God.

Day 3   Submitted Emotions

SEEK GOD

Pray over and meditate on this week's memory verse. Ask Father to give you wisdom and revelation.

OBTAIN TRUTH

I remember a time when I couldn't feel God's presence. I also remember feeling like God would distance Himself from me when I wasn't obedient. I would feel so guilty.

I believed that my sins were too bad for God and, so, He gave up on me! Seriously, I thought this. The more my thoughts consumed me, the guiltier I felt. The more I thought, the more my emotions increased; so I felt lonely, depressed, and abandoned.

Thankfully I've learned that this was not the truth. I cannot trust my feelings as evidence that God is or isn't within me. I have to establish fully my trust in Him and in His Word that He will never leave me. (Matthew 28:20). I have to trust this truth regardless of how I feel.

How did this emotional downward spiral that I experienced even start?

It began with a thought. My emotional pain erupted from a thought. That's all it takes – one thought to start a chain reaction of negative emotions and more damaging thoughts.

This is why Jesus tells us to control our thoughts. In 2 Corinthians 10:5 the Bible teaches us that we have the power to "take captive every thought to make it obedient to Christ." Once a thought is conceived, our emotions will respond accordingly unless we renew our minds!

Title a journal page "Abiding Emotions." The Bible gives us truths and tools to train our soul (our mind, will, and emotions) to abide by the Spirit of God. Read one or all of today's passages: 1 Corinthians 9:25-27, 2 Corinthians10:5, Matthew 6:33, 1 Samuel 16:1, 1 Samuel 30:6, 1 Samuel 31:13, Galatians 5:24-26, Colossians 3, Isaiah 26:3, Isaiah 54:17, 1 Peter 1:8, Proverbs 23:7, Deuteronomy 30:19, Romans 8:6, Romans 10:17, and Zechariah 4:6.

Write a list of practical things that the Bible teaches you to do in order to get your emotions to submit to the Spirit.

Take time to write down any emotions and thoughts that spiral you down into places that are set against God's truth. For example:

"I'm insecure."
"I'm unlovable."
"I'm alone."

Take the lies captive by God's truth and make them obedient to Christ. Next write down the truth, as in the following examples, beside your negative thoughts:

"I'm secure!"
"I'm loved!"
"I'm in Christ, and Christ is in me!"

ABIDE

Many of us are working hard to try to be good enough to abide in Christ, but it's not by our efforts and moral strength that we attain that goal; it's by His Spirit. Goodness is about Him working in and through us – not us striving on our own. We have to change our thinking here and throw our lame attempts (which can only bring self-righteousness) to the side. Then the Spirit of God can move in all His might.

Zechariah 4:6 says, "…Not by might nor by power, but by my Spirit,' says the LORD Almighty."

Self-effort compartmentalizes God.

Out of a sense of duty or habit, for instance, you might have your quiet time and then walk away from it to live the rest of your day without another thought of God. Your day just became too overwrought with tasks and ongoing distractions. If this is you, please realize that you don't have to live this way! It is possible to have meaningfully connected fellowship with God throughout the busiest of days!

How is this done? Minute by minute. You learn to sustain an awareness of His presence with you. Child of God, recognize that His presence won't depart you! Once you've maintained this realization, begin to delight and rejoice in it. The overflow of this truth will create an amazing child to Daddy relationship.

Does this seem overly simplistic to you? You have things to do – work, kids, study, appointments, and so on. Each of us can list a thousand things we need to do! Let me explain how this has worked out in my family:

This summer, as a family, we focused on Isaiah 26:3, "You keep him in perfect peace whose mind is stayed on You because he trusts in You."

Before we focused our attention on Isaiah, I saw idleness in the attitudes of my kids.

So here's how, practically, we took idleness of thought and kept our minds on God: I started spending more time in the details of what my children were doing. We used the acronym for SOAR to continually focus us on God:

- **S**eek God – Pray aloud together every morning.
- **O**btain Truth –Read the Bible at the start of each day together.
- **A**sk questions – How did you see God today?
- **R**espond to God – Praised and thanked God throughout the day.

This gave my family a fresh perspective. We now see everything through new eyes! Everything that my kids read, do, or look at is now an opportunity for them to see God in a fresh way. It is helping all of us to keep our thoughts on God!

As Isaiah 26:3 moved from our heads to our hearts, we began to see a complete change in our family's imaginations, attitudes, actions, and topics of conversation.

When you understand how much God loves you (if you are not sure, go back to Week Eight, "I Am Loved," in Obtain Truth), it becomes easy to keep your mind on Him because He loves you so much. He loves you unconditionally and will always be with you (Matthew 28:20).

If you aren't experiencing perfect peace (Romans 8:6), try our SOAR acronym. Jesus is the Prince of Peace!

Day 4   Encourage Yourself

SEEK GOD

Ask God for the heart and eyes of David so that you can more fully understand your identity in Christ.

OBTAIN TRUTH

Read 1 Samuel 30:1-20.

Divide a journal page in half. On one half use the title "Worldly Response" and on the other write "Godly Response."

As you read this chapter, write down how you see the men in this story respond to their crisis situation.

In 1 Samuel 30:6, David encouraged himself in the Lord. I cannot imagine coming home and finding my spouse, family, home, belongings, and town completely gone. Imagine the devastation.

What thoughts caused David to be encouraged and enabled him to encourage his men?

Use your imagination and write down, on a new journal page, "How David Encouraged Himself." Contemplate your answers all throughout the day or even for a few days. Then come back to this journal page and jot down your additional thoughts.

ABIDE

What circumstance is before you right now? You have a choice—two ways to respond. You can choose the path of David's men, or you can choose the path of David. Which will you choose? Why?

Ask God to reveal to you how to respond to your circumstance with a godly response rather than a worldly response.

Our family has recently been under a major spiritual attack. We have been applying 1 Samuel 30:6 to our daily life. We have written down all of the wonderful things that God has done for our family – the salvations of family and friends, the miracles we have experienced, and other things that remind us of God's love for us. We posted each wonder of God on our wall.

Now we can pray and thank God as we look at what He has done. Every time we feel discouraged, we can easily recall that God is for us and not against us. And every single time we are completely encouraged! It's absolutely true that in the presence of the Lord is the fullness of joy (Psalms 16:11)!

Continue reciting your memory verse aloud. As your heart and mind remain on the Lord, He will keep you in perfect peace.

Day 5   Fear Not

SEEK GOD

Pray over the memory verse this morning. Ask God to help your soul learn to abide in Him as Paul's did!

OBTAIN TRUTH

Read John 14. Title a journal page "Jesus' last instructions to me."

John 14 includes part of Jesus' last words to His disciples. He is getting ready to be crucified and wants His disciples to be prepared for the upcoming days. He wants them to be strong and not be moved by the circumstances that they will experience. Jesus wants them to stand firm in the truth that he has been teaching them for the last three years.

As you read the text, write down Jesus' last words to His disciples. Keep in mind that they are also words for you.

ABIDE

Jesus commanded us in John 14:1 and John 14:27 not to allow our emotions and a negative thought-life to control our behavior.

Just before He was crucified, He instructed the disciples not to let their hearts be troubled. What? They were getting ready to see their leader, friend, and teacher crucified on a cross. In the immediate moment, it would look as if the past three years of their life were wasted. They didn't have a full understanding of God's plan yet.

Jesus tried to explain to them what was going to happen. He was giving them a command to "not let their hearts be troubled." Take another look at His words:

> "Peace I leave with you; my peace I give you. I do not give to you as the world gives. Do not let your hearts be troubled and do not be afraid." (John 14:27)

The word troubled in the original Greek text means "to stir" or to "agitate." We could paraphrase Jesus' instruction as, "Do not allow your mind and emotions to be stirred up in an anxious, fearful knot. Receive peace, *my* peace; I offer it to you!"

Check out John 14:27 in the Amplified Bible:

"Peace I leave with you; My [own] peace I now give and bequeath to you. Not as the world gives do I give to you. Do not let your hearts be troubled, neither let them be afraid. [Stop allowing yourselves to be agitated and disturbed; and do not permit yourselves to be fearful and intimidated and cowardly and unsettled.]"

Admit it; you have experienced emotional rollercoasters. Maybe this is because you looked at your circumstances rather than looking at God. When you dwell on the trials and problems in front of you, they seem larger than God.

Never depend on your own understanding. Instead, trust in your God, who has complete understanding.

The disciples didn't completely understand. If you read further in John, you'll see that they leaned on their own assumptions and perceptions. They relied on what they saw with their eyes more than they trusted the words of Jesus!

They should have trusted Jesus' instructions!

How is it possible to lose someone significant in your life and "not allow your heart to be troubled or not afraid"?

I don't have this figured out yet. What I do know is that Jesus would not give a command that we could not accomplish. He will always provide a way through His power and grace.

And as we know our Father more and more, we are able to tap into an endless supply of joy and peace—no matter what comes our way.

ABIDE – Week Four
God's Power Living in You (with Sheri)

Memory Verse:

> For the kingdom of God is not a matter of talk but of power.
> (1 Corinthians 4:20)

Video Review: http://www.soarwithgod.com/Abide/Abide.html

> "In this world you will have trouble. But take heart! I have overcome the world."
> (John 16:33)

What trouble are you facing today?

_____

When trouble comes, there are two ways to handle it:

1. Abide in *your* strength or abide in God's power. "But he (Jesus) said to me, 'My grace is sufficient for you, for my power is made perfect in weakness'" (2 Corinthians 12:9)

2. "Finally, be strong in the Lord and in his mighty power." (Ephesians 6:10)

How to Abide in God's Power

- Realize that you have God's power.
- Know what His authority gives you.
- Stay in His presence.
- "He who dwells in the shelter of the Most High will rest in the shadow of the Almighty." (Psalm 91:1)
- Exercise what you have been given.

> In the same way, faith by itself, if it is not accompanied by action, is dead. (James 2:17)

What trouble are you facing today?

Jesus' Name is Above Every Name!

Therefore God exalted him to the highest place and gave him the name that is above every name, that at the name of Jesus every knee should bow, in heaven and on earth and under the earth, 1 and every tongue acknowledge that Jesus Christ is Lord, to the glory of God the Father. (Philippians 2:9-11)

Day 1   WWW.DO

"Faith does not operate in the realm of the possible. There is no glory for God in that which is humanly possible. Faith begins where man's power ends." — George Mueller

Before we start, we must begin with this truth: Abiding authority is never about results; it's about relationship.

If you are seeking God merely for results, you will end up reducing this section of the study to trying to find the "magic formula." There is *no* such formula. Formulas use manipulation and we cannot manipulate God.

Jesus never taught the disciples a formula for abiding in their authority. He just told them that they had His authority. They didn't always use this authority victoriously because they were mere humans. And like them, we will also run into dealing with our own weaknesses and unbelief.

The authority Christ gave us to do His work for His glory on this earth still exists. It lives in you! To find out how much power is available in Christ, take the time to seek Him personally in both prayer and the Word. Don't go through life without knowing what you have in Christ!

When you know whose you are, who you are, and what you have, you will know what to do.

I call this "WWW.DO!"

Whose – **W**ho – **W**hat – DO!

Let's look at Gideon's life. God tells Gideon *whose* He is and *what* he has, in Judges 6:12: "The Lord is with you." In the same verse, God tells Gideon *who* he is—"mighty warrior."

Gideon had the Living God with him as his weapon!

God also told Gideon what He would do. Because Gideon had the confidence of knowing whose he was, who he was, and what he had, he knew that he was able to *do* what God called him to do. Judges 6:16 declares, "You [Gideon] will strike down all the Midianites together."

I spoke with my friend John, who recently retired from the police force. As an officer, John knew that he was given authority by the city and state to enforce the law. He had to step into his identity as a policeman, know the weapons he possessed, and know that he was operating in the authority of the government. Once he understood these essentials, he knew what to do in his position of authority.

WHOSE you are – Do not forget whose you are! You are God's adopted child (Ephesians 1:4-5)!

As a child, regardless of whether your parents are good or bad, you love them because you belong to them. You learn to trust them if they are loving and trustworthy.

This is the same with God. Growing closer to Him causes your trust in Him to deepen. You begin to see that His love for you and plans for you are far beyond your understanding. Pursue God. Continually seek to know Him better. Stay in love with God and your trust will be in Him alone!

When you know *whose* you are, suddenly you will know *who* you are.

WHO you are – As God's child, you are a co-heir with Jesus Christ! You are secure, holy, and blameless in the sight of God. Go to the Obtain Truth study if you want to know more.

My friend John knew who he was. He was a law enforcer. He knew what to do when he saw someone break the law.

When you know *who* you are you begin to grasp *what* you have.

WHAT you have – You have the same Spirit abiding in you as abided in Jesus! You have faith and life-giving resurrection power abiding in and for you. You have all that you need for life and godliness through the Holy Spirit. You just need to know how to utilize what is yours!

John was given weapons to carry out law enforcement. His greatest weapon, he said, was his uniform. Citizens knew when they saw the uniform that they needed to abide by the law or they were in trouble.

In the same way, your spiritual enemy can recognize the authority of Jesus Christ in you. Remember that you have the armor of God as your uniform.

When you know what you *have*, you will know what to *do*.

DO – John knew that his position gave him specific authority by the city and state. They informed him of the weapons he'd obtained and how to employ them in order to carry out what he was trained to accomplish.

When you know whose you are, who you are, and what you have, you will know what to do. The Holy Spirit will guide and instruct you.

The abiding authority that you have in and through Christ is never about you or the results. It's about a loving God that provides everything for His children and His eternal purposes. We in turn glorify Him by using the authority we have been given to do what He calls us to do!

Day 2   God Has My Back

SEEK GOD

Seek God with all your heart, soul, mind, and strength today. Review the memory verse and pray it over yourself. This is your calling! Ask God to help you see with opened eyes and to hear His truth in a new way today!

OBTAIN TRUTH

The scriptures today are very powerful! Read and examine them closely. Let them soak in. Pray for greater understanding.

Many people have learned Bible verses by memory, but they haven't begun to live the Scriptures out in their own lives. They don't know the freedom and victory that child-like faith can bring.

Read Luke 10:17-21, James 4:7, 1 John 4:4:1-6, and Isaiah 54:17.

In your journal, write down what your authority in Christ is under the title "My Authority in Christ."

ABIDE

Faith comes from hearing God's Word (Romans 10:17). The world, news, friends, family, and other sources will tell you that you just have to make the best of your circumstances or that you should prepare for the worst-case scenario.

The truth is that you have something the world doesn't: you have the gift of the Holy Spirit dwelling within. You have same power that raised Christ from the dead!

You can be victorious and overcome in every trial. When you are in Christ, no weapon formed against you will succeed (Isaiah 54:17)!

Many people quote this verse, but they leave out the second half: "and you will silence every tongue that accuses you."

In other words, God has a role: He will turn every weapon used against you for good. You have a role: Silence all accusers. But how and what does this mean?

This does not necessarily mean that you should defend yourself. God is your defender. To me, it means that if someone (like your evil adversary) tells you that you are no-good, sick, poor, or defeated, you must remember that God's Word is the truth. You need to know the promises of God and agree with them. It's important for you to discern when lies and physical facts are spoken against or contrary to the Word of God.

When trials, suffering and criticism come your way, I want you to see that God in you is far greater than anything that comes against you! None of these weapons will win. Remember the wave story from the video this week? The waves cannot defeat you when you know you are walking with the One greater than any trouble.

Allow your thoughts to dwell on how gargantuan your God is rather than on how monstrous your problem is!

One day I realized that I sometimes actually believed my problems were more robust than my God. That is sheer idolatry. I worshipped my problems, not God. It was evidence by the amount of time I spent talking about my problems. This revelation penetrated me like a knife when I realized it. The truth is God has my back – and He has yours. He is monumentally larger than anything you and I are facing.

This truth has changed me! I pray that it changes you, too.

> *"We have to pray with our eyes on God, not on the difficulties."*
>
> — Oswald Chambers

Day 3   Open My Eyes

SEEK GOD

Pray that the eyes of your heart are opened to understand truly what it means to be an adopted child of God. Pray that you will understand what belongs to you as His child. Review your memory verse and pray it over yourself.

OBTAIN TRUTH

Read Ephesians 1:17-23, Colossians 2:10, Matthew 10:1and 8, Mark 11:20-26, Mark 16:9-18, Isaiah 40:29, Genesis 1:26-28, and John 14:8-14.

Wow! As I prepare this and pour over these verses, I am fired up! I hope you will be, too! Go through each verse attentively. In your journal, write down what is yours under the title "What I Have in Christ."

ABIDE

Meditate on your notes from today's lesson. I pray that your heart will experience a greater freedom from the knowledge of God's truth.

"If you then, evil as you are, know how to give good and advantageous gifts to your children, how much more will your Father Who is in heaven [perfect as He is] give good and advantageous things to those who keep on asking Him!"
(Matthew 7:11 AMP)

Day 4   Submit to God

SEEK GOD

Seek God and ask Him for a deeper revelation and understanding of your abiding authority.

OBTAIN TRUTH

Read Mark 7:1-13, Matthew 13:53-58, Matthew 8:23-27, and James 3:13-16 and 4:1-16.

Notice specifically that James 4:7 says, "Resist the devil and he will flee from you." I have heard this verse quoted, in part, many times but most leave out what precedes this instruction: "Submit yourselves to God." Do resist the enemy, but remember that the power to overcome the enemy comes from your submission to God Almighty!

Your actions can neutralize the power of God in your life. Dig into James 3:13-16 and title a journal page "Ineffective Authority."

Write down issues that can cause your authority in Christ to be ineffective or neutralized.

Title another journal page "Effective Living." Read John 5:19, John 8:28-29, John 14:8-16, John 15:5, and Ephesians 5:1.

What made Jesus' authority effective (besides the fact that He is the Son of God)? Why is your authority in Christ effective? Write down your answers.

ABIDE

Soak in the following verse and your notes from this lesson to renew your mind.

Blessed is the man who does not walk in the counsel of the wicked or stand in the way of sinners or sit in the seat of mockers. But his delight is in the law of the Lord, and on is law he meditates day and night. He is like a tree planted by streams of water, which yields its fruit in season and whose leaf does not wither. Whatever he does prospers. (Psalm 1:1-3)

Day 5   Incomparable Power

SEEK GOD

Ask God to reveal to you personally the authority He has given you. Thank Him for it.

OBTAIN TRUTH

Read Matthew 10 and Luke 9:1-17.

Title a journal page "My Mandate." As you read, write down what authority or jurisdiction was given to the disciples. Recognize that *you* are a disciple of Jesus! You have the *same* authority.

Write down the calling and authorization that the disciples were given.

ABIDE

Carefully consider the verses that you've just read. Some Christians believe that the power and miracles of God have somehow ended after the days of the "Early Church." But is this a truth revealed to us through Scripture? Is this what Jesus taught? Have an honest look and allow the Holy Spirit to guide you into all truth.

You are a disciple (a student-follower) of Jesus; so imagine yourself in this scene with Him. Ask yourself these questions:

* How were able to perform miracles?
* Where did they get their authority?
* How did they know how to use it?
* How did they have the confidence to go out and preach the good news?
* What does Ephesians 1:18-23 mean to you?

What if our lack of seeing the greater works of God were due to our doubt and unbelief? As you write down your thoughts, ask God to reveal to you His truth.

Day 6   Wall of Miracles

SEEK GOD

Prepare your heart before your Father to receive all that He desires to teach you.

OBTAIN TRUTH

Read Acts 3:1-16.

My family has been learning to abide in our authority in Christ for a few years now. Sometimes we abide in our authority, and others times we don't. Let's just say, we have not arrived.

This past summer my husband casted vision for our family. We were to believe and rely on God more and not be swayed into doubt by our circumstances. Because of this we witnessed over eighty miracles! It was an amazing journey!

We weren't successful in every occasion, but we experienced God's love and power in an amazing way.

Recently my six-year-old child has been under a spiritual attack.

We used John 14:11 to encourage her: "...or at least believe on the evidence of the miracles themselves." We recounted all of the powerful acts of God that we had seen in the past year. My child's faith was immediately encouraged. We realized in that moment how imperative it is to remember constantly the works of God!

We built a "Wall of Miracles" in our home. This is where we write down a work of God on a post-it note and stick it on our miracle board. When we get discouraged or become complacent, we can quickly review the wall and praise God for all that He has done. Talk about encouraging!

ABIDE

This week, build an authority wall, answered-prayer wall, or miracle wall for your home.

Use some sticky notes or a white board. You may want to sit down with a friend or your family and go through your study notes from this week together before you start.

Place your answered prayers and miracles on your wall or board. Celebrate the faithful provision of God in your life.

CRAVE

If you are truly hungry to understand more about the abiding power of Jesus, I recommend further study in God's Word. It's going to take time, but I believe that your faith will be strengthened, your eyes will be opened, and you will be forever transformed by this challenge.

You can pick one or more of the passages below or read through Matthew, Mark, Luke, and John. These are referred to as the four gospels. They depict the life and ministry of Christ.

- Matthew 8
- Matthew 9
- Matthew 12
- Mark 5:25-29
- Mark 10:46-52
- Luke 18:35-43
- Matthew 20:29-34
- John 5:1-9
- Luke 6:17-19

Title a journal page "Authority." As you read, write down what authority was given to the disciples. Recognize that *you* are a disciple of Jesus! You have the *same* Authority.

Title one journal page with the heading "Miracles."

Answer the following questions:

- How did the miracle occur? (Was it a touch, a word, or something else? Are you unsure?)
- How many people were healed?
- What did the person do to receive the miracle?
- Create your own question here.

ABIDE – Week Five
Keeping Hope Alive (with Amy)

Memory Verse:

> But hope that is seen is no hope at all. Who hopes for what they already have? But if we hope for what we do not yet have, we wait for it patiently. (Romans 8:24-25)

Video Review: http://www.soarwithgod.com/Abide/Abide.html

Because we are one with Jesus, we should live with an _____.

> May the God of hope fill you with all joy and peace, as you trust in him, so that you may overflow with hope by the power of the Holy Spirit. (Romans 15:13)

What does it mean to hope? Is hope the same as faith?

Faith is confident _____.

Hope is confident _____.

Is your hope really in God? On what or whom do you depend?

Circle all that apply:

Myself – my abilities – money - my job – my experiences – medicine – an "expert" – books – food – my relationship(s) – exercising – a chemical substance – weekends / vacations – a hobby – possessions –other: _____

We put our _____ in what we _____.

We _____ what we _____.

The disciples needed to KNOW Jesus more!

> Jesus was sleeping at the back of the boat with his head on a cushion. The disciples woke him up, shouting, "Teacher, don't you care that we're going to drown?" When Jesus woke up, he rebuked the wind and said to the waves, "Silence! Be still!" Suddenly the wind stopped, and there was a great calm. Then he asked them, "Why are you afraid? Do you still have no faith?" The disciples were absolutely terrified. "Who is this man?" they asked each other. "Even the wind and waves obey him!" (Mark 4:35-41)

Abraham knew God!

> Against all hope, Abraham in hope believed and so became the father of many nations, just as it had been said to him, "So shall your offspring be." Without weakening in his faith, he faced the fact that his body was as good as dead-since he was about a hundred years old-and that Sarah's womb was also dead. Yet he did not waver through unbelief regarding the promise of God, but was strengthened in his faith and gave glory to God, being fully persuaded that God had power to do what he had promised. (Romans 4:18-21)

When I place my hope in GOD...

...I can patiently and confidently _____!

Additional Scripture references include Romans 5:2-5, Hebrews 6:15, James 5:7-11, and Habakkuk 3:17-19.

Day 1   Put Your Hope in God

SEEK GOD

Recite this week's memory verse aloud twice.

Draw near to God in prayer, your heart filled with a confident and patient hope. Enjoy the richness of His fellowship.

OBTAIN TRUTH

The prophet Isaiah, in Isaiah 40, gives a meaningful perspective on the greatness of God and the frailty of man. We also see the compassion of God towards foolish and wayward hearts.

Read Isaiah 40:25-31 and compile a list in your journal under the heading, "Because God Is... I Can Expect..." You will discover what you can expect from your mighty God! If time allows, read through the entire chapter for further impact.

ABIDE

Are you more often full of hope or full of worry and fear about the future?

Maybe, like the psalmist in Psalm 42:5, you need to talk to yourself and remember that God is good! Try saying, "Why, my soul, are you downcast? Why so disturbed within me? Put your hope in God, for I will yet praise him, my Savior and my God."

This is living by faith and seeing with eyes of hope! Don't be emotionally tossed around by life's circumstances. Plant your hope and your expectations in God!

Allow the truth of who God is to correct all of your faithless deliberating. Write down anything and everything that is disturbing your heart and mind. Align any defeated attitudes with renewed, faith-filled expectations because of who God is.

You will discover that placing your hope in God truly does renew your strength.

Day 2   Eager Anticipation

SEEK GOD

Recite this week's memory verse aloud twice. Seek to grasp the greatness of God at a greater depth. Wait patiently in hope for what you do not yet have.

OBTAIN TRUTH

Read Romans 8:18-39.

Prepare your journal with the title "In Christ, I Can Expect..."

Read carefully and produce a list of the hopes that you have. You don't want to miss a single nugget of truth today! Get ready to be blessed as you realize what you have through Christ.

ABIDE

Some have defined hope as an expectation of coming good. I like this definition. Through our salvation we have an unimaginable wonderful future!

I (Amy) have always loved telling my children about their eternal future. I want them to grasp that this world is not their home—that one day (whether they are asleep or awake, living or dead) their Savior will come in the clouds, and they will fly to meet Him in the air. I want them to remain expectant and ready. We all need to abide in eternal anticipation.

In Ephesians 1:18 and 19, the apostle Paul prayed a heartfelt prayer for us, "that the eyes of your heart may be enlightened in order that you may know the hope to which he has called you, the riches of his glorious inheritance in his holy people, and his incomparably great power for us who believe."

Pray this prayer to God now as your own heart's desire.

Look over the list that you made from Romans. Steep your mind in the reality of your sure hope. Ask God to enlighten and flood your whole life with these truths.

Write out a prayer in response to all that God is revealing to you.

Day 3   Happy Trials to You

SEEK GOD

Recite this week's memory verse aloud twice.

Draw near to God in prayer, your heart filled with a confident and patient hope. Enjoy the richness of His fellowship.

OBTAIN TRUTH

We are going to examine our hope in the midst of trials and suffering today.

Read James 1:2-8, Romans 5:1-11, and 1 Peter 1:3-7, and complete the statement "I can rejoice because I have..." In your journal, record a list of what you've been given.

ABIDE

"Rejoice in our sufferings" and "consider it pure joy" when in various trials? Does this sound a little crazy to you? It is unusual, but it is God's prescribed way for spiritual maturity.

I would not be the Christ-follower I am today if it were not for my painful trials. Every battle with my sin, fear, sickness, rejection, loss, and daily problems has allowed me to become more like Christ Jesus.

When our faith is in the fire of life's trials and we press on, placing our trust in God, it purifies us and makes us more like Him. Trials can cause our hope to soar because we see the truth of His faithfulness at work in and around us. Romans 12:12 says, "Be joyful in hope, patient in affliction, faithful in prayer."

Are you facing your struggles with patience, joy, and prayer? You can. You can confidently expect God to work out good in all things for you, His beloved child (Romans 8:28).

If you are not walking in peace and joy, you need to reset your mind. Renew your attitude with the truth of who God is!

The other day I was terribly disappointed—no, I was fed up. Done. I'd had enough. I had been waiting for God to answer my prayer to heal my recurring bladder-infections. When I say waiting, I mean I have been waiting for the past nine or so years! Well, this day there was no rejoicing in all circumstances going on in my heart. I wanted an end to my problem right then!

I had done everything I understood the Bible advised in order to receive healing as well as prayerfully gone to doctors, taken their meds, taken heaps of natural remedies, and listened to and applied "helpful" advice, all to no avail.

God is so good! He is so patient and generous with me. And I am giddy with renewed hope! Why? Did I receive my healing? Maybe. I'm not sure about my tomorrows. But I know that God will be with me in them. My healing may have come. If so, praise God! Even if it is not readily evident now, I expect that all things are working out for my good and for His glory. His grace has *always* been sufficient for me.

My joy left that day because I became impatient. Not any more. I am waiting full of expectation. My God is everything I need.

Wait, loved one. Wait patiently on Him. Choose to walk in His goodness and strength. You can live full of joy because you know, depend on, and place all hope in your faithful God.

Day 4   Eternal Eyes

SEEK GOD

Recite this week's memory verse aloud twice.

Pursue God in prayer with your heart confident in the hope that you have. Savor the wonder of His fellowship with you.

OBTAIN TRUTH

Read 2 Corinthians 4:7–5:10.

Use the journal entry "In every trial, I have..." and fill your page with every glorious promise that is yours through Christ.

ABIDE

It can be difficult to fix your mind on the eternal when the temporary is so real and ever-present. My days are loaded up with fun and meaningful moments as well as with monotonous and dutiful routine. Next throw in the burden of life's daily struggles. Where can one find the time to consider the eternal?

Keeping your eyes on the unseen is a matter of the heart. When your passion for God is thriving, you will overflow with eternal thoughts. You won't be able to hold them back! The trouble is that your circumstances can bombard and distract you from your First Love. Don't allow it! Stay aware of the roadblocks that stand in the way of your priority relationship.

When a problem arises, I have learned to ask the following questions:

- Will this matter in 100 years?
- What is the eternal significance of this?
- Father God, what do You want to teach me through this?
- Father, what do You want me to do?

These kinds of questions place everything in perspective so that wisdom begins to take precedence.

What do you need to do to keep your mind and heart on Christ?

Write your burdens down in your journal. Beside each burden, write what you will do to keep your mind on your hope in Christ.

Day 5   Sure and Certain

SEEK GOD

Recite this week's memory verse aloud twice.

Draw near to God in prayer, your heart filled with a confident and patient hope. Rejoice in the blessings of His fellowship.

OBTAIN TRUTH

Today we're going to take a look at some men who had abundant faith and hope in God.

Take your journal and use the ABC study method. Read Genesis 22:1-18, Daniel 3, and Hebrews 6:9-20.

"A" is for "**A** title" – How would you summarize, in a title form, the passage that you read?

"B" is for "**B**est verse" – What was your favorite verse? There is no right or wrong answer.

"C" is for "**C**alling" – Does this passage call you to live out a certain task?

ABIDE

Hebrews 10:23 declares, "Let us hold tightly without wavering to the hope we affirm, for God can be trusted to keep his promise."

Hold tightly to your hope. Hold on without hesitation. God can be trusted!

- Is there any part of you that lacks complete trust in God?
- What generates worry and anxiety? Write every worry that comes to mind.

A lack of trust and an anxious heart are sure evidence of a weak faith and the need to know God more intimately.

I want to have the kind of faith and hope that Abraham and the three Hebrew men had, don't you? They knew God well, and they had resolute, strong faith.

If you are pursuing God and living according to His Word, then you are headed in the right direction! God wants you to look to Him with total trust and patiently wait for His perfect work to be performed. *Expect* it.

Hebrews 11:1 defines what faith is: "Now faith is being sure of what we hope for and certain of what we do not see."

CRAVE

Read through Genesis 22 again. Using the title "Abraham, Man of Faith," create a list of every faith-filled action that Abraham performed.

ABIDE – Week Six
Faith Expressed by Love (with Amy and Sheri)

Memory Verse:

> "As the Father has loved me, so have I loved you. Now remain in my love."
> (John 15:9)

Video Review: http://www.soarwithgod.com/Abide/Abide.html

Day 1   Agape Love

SEEK GOD

Seek God in prayer and ask Him to reveal to you the depth and breadth of His intimate love.

OBTAIN TRUTH

Read John 15:9-17 and 1 John 4:9-10.

God's love for you is immeasurable! Title a journal page "God's Love for Me." As you read today's passages, write down all that God reveals about His love for you.

ABIDE

When we first started the SOAR bible study, the Abide section was called "Agape." We initially chose this because if we have an abiding problem, then we really have a love problem.

John 14:15 reads, "If you love me, keep my commands."

If you are not walking by God's voice and literally obeying His every word to you, this verse reveals the source of your lack of obedience—your lack of love for God. The solution for a lack of love is to do things that bring intimacy. Don't take God's love for granted. Take time to gaze on His beauty through prayer, meditation, and reading the Word. Reflect on the grace, forgiveness, and love that He has lavished on you. Consider the kind of love that God has for you.

Not all love is the same:

Eros, phileo, and agape are all Greek words for love.

After you learn about these three Greek words for love, ask God to open your eyes so that you know His immense love for you.

Eros is a romantic kind of love. It is dependent upon the situation and perception, not truth. This kind of love is fickle since it depends on circumstances. This is not a biblical word used for God's love.

Phileo love is the kind of love we experience in friendships, family, and fellowship with people we enjoy. It is having a feeling of affection in the heart for those we care about. Phileo is one of the New Testament biblical words used for human love.

Agape love is the purest form of love. It is not based on a temporary feeling but, rather, is rooted in a commitment to love. It is not limited to a situation, circumstance, or your perception. This love is often referred to as "unconditional love."

Eros and phileo types of love are significantly enriched and empowered by God if agape love is our foundation. Responding out of agape love with others is deciding to love regardless of treatment or circumstance.

Agape love is how God loves us!

> But God demonstrates his own love for us in this: While we were still sinners,
> Christ died for us. (Romans 5:8)

Understanding that God's love toward you is not based on a feeling or on what you do for Him, but rather His decision to love you regardless, will transform your life!

We can never earn God's love – not today, tomorrow, or any day! The way you love God, others, and yourself will never be the same after you understand this simple (yet profound) truth!

How do you abide in love? You choose to do so. You commit to agape love—a love that is not based on feelings or circumstances. Will you do this today?

Receive God's love for you. Choose agape love!

Day 2　Know God, Know Love

SEEK GOD

Ask the Father to reveal His love more to you today.

OBTAIN TRUTH

Read 1 John 4:7-21.

We often define love as based on a feeling, but God's love is different. Read today's text and then divide a journal page in half. On the left side, write "How I Define Love" and produce a list of your own ideas of love. Next, on the right side of the page, describe "How God Defines Love" from the 1 John passage.

ABIDE

Jesus declares clearly in 1 John 4, "Whoever does not love does not know God, because God is love." If you are like me, this statement can come across as extremely strong and disturbing. I have had my share of unloving thoughts and actions toward people.

What exactly is Jesus saying here? Is He really saying that when I don't speak or act out of love that I don't know God? As piercing as it is, I believe the answer is yes. Jesus' blunt statement leaves little room or need for interpretation.

When my first daughter was born, I realized that there were not enough books or advice to prepare me for the first time the doctors laid her across my lap. I am fairly sure that I said out loud, "What am I suppose to do with her now?"

Before long I could tell what she needed by the tone of her cry. As I began to know her more intimately, I naturally knew how to demonstrate to her the love and care that she required. Growing older, she quickly learned that her daddy and me need her obedience in order for us to guide and protect her. Love is beautifully given and received when we respectfully submit to one another.

Just as a parent and child grow in intimacy, you should strive to gain a deeper understanding of God. You'll discover how worthy of love He is, and you will humbly desire to do what pleases Him. I believe that we all need to hear the message of "know God more" again and again. The SOAR study repeatedly challenges you to give God secret time in both quality and quantity each day. You'll soon stand in awe of how much your heart has become like His.

Day 3   My Father's Eyes

SEEK GOD

Ask your Heavenly Father today to help you see people the way He sees them. Ask Him to help you love others the way He loves them.

OBTAIN TRUTH

> The elder, to my dear friend Gaius, whom I love in the truth. (3 John 1:1)

This verse blows me away! John didn't say, "I love you for all the wonderful things you have done." He didn't say, "I have deep feelings toward you."

No. He said, "Whom I love in the truth."

What is the "truth"? The Truth is Jesus and the Word of God.

What he is saying here, essentially, is that he loves Gaius through God's eyes. He loves him because he sees him as God sees him. Are you grasping this?

John had to know how much God loved him in order to love others with God's love. You and I need to realize wholly His love for us, too, if we want the God kind of love to pour out of us.

Let's review how God views you (from SOAR: Obtain Truth):

- You are blessed in the heavenly realms with every spiritual blessing in Christ. (Ephesians 1:3)
- He chose you in Him before the creation of the world. (Ephesians 1:4)
- You are holy and blameless in His sight. (Ephesians 1:4)
- In His love, He predestined you to be adopted through Jesus Christ.
- He has freely given you His grace. (Ephesians 1:6)
- You have redemption in Him through Christ. (Ephesians 1:7)
- You are forgiven. (Ephesians 1:7)
- He has made known the mystery of His will to you. (Ephesians 1:9)
- You are chosen and have been predestined according to His plan. (Ephesians 1:11)
- You were included in Christ when you heard the word of truth, the Gospel of your salvation. When you believed, you were marked with a seal, the promised Holy Spirit, who is a deposit guaranteeing your inheritance (Ephesians 1:14).
- God has vast love for you (Ephesians 2:4).
- You have been saved by His grace. (Ephesians 2:5)
- You have been saved by grace, through faith—and this not from yourself, it is the gift of God—not by works. (Ephesians 2:8-9)
- You are God's masterpiece. (Ephesians 2:10)

Are you beginning to see the point? John knew how much God loved him. Because of that, he was able show love to Gaius and others with God's extreme kind of love.

ABIDE

Learn to see yourself and others through God's eyes.

Thank God for His amazing love for you. Choose to see others through God's love.

When someone cuts you off in traffic, instead of responding with rudeness or hatefulness, consider responding with how God sees him or her: "Jesus loves them so much that He already died for this sin. Because of that I have the power in Him to give them mercy."

You may be wondering how to treat unbelievers. Do you give them mercy? Do you chase them down and point out their sin? I presume not. God loves all of the people in the world. Jesus died for the sins of the whole world ... not just yours (1 John 2:2). God desires all people to be saved!

> God our Savior, who wants all people to be saved and to come to a knowledge of the truth. (1 Timothy 2:1)

We need to be His hands and feet by choosing to love all people. Your actions could be the first encounter with Jesus that many unsaved people have. They will see Jesus and know Him through your love for them and for your brothers and sisters. They should want what we have!

Our attitude should be, "I choose to bless those who mistreat me and do everything in love."

When you are tempted to become offended or angry with someone, remember that you are called to forgive as Christ has forgiven you.

This will shut your lips in a hurry.

When I began to see others through God's eyes, everything changed. I didn't see my husband's faults through eyes of criticism (although sometimes I still do), but rather, I look at him knowing that God views him as a masterpiece! When I do this, it *changes me*! It changes how I respond to him!

When I began to love others based on truth, I became a mighty encourager! People tell me all the time what a superb encourager I am. I don't really see it, but I do see people whom God loves. I just want to be a vessel to help others see God's love for them!

I like to encourage people based on truth, not on performance. The world shows love and encouragement based on performance. When you are performing by the world's standards, they may encourage and love you. When you are not measuring up, you get a massive dose of discouragement. That's not God's kind of love, and it shouldn't be ours either.

We get enough performance-based, circumstantial love from the world!

Choose to be a Christian with God's love permeating every word that you speak, every activity you do, and each thought to which you give power.

I want every believer to know how much God loves them and who they are in Christ! *Why?*

Because when you truly understand the truth, you truly can begin to love God and others as John loved Gaius—and to love who you are becoming in Him!

"We love JESUS best when we love OTHERS well."— Lisa Bevere

Begin to practice keeping your thoughts on what is true about God's love for you and others. It will change your life!

Day 4   Choose Love

SEEK GOD

Allow yourself time to be still before the Father. Quiet yourself and ask Him to fill you with His fruit of love.

OBTAIN TRUTH

Read 1 Corinthians 13.

Our study of abiding love would not be complete without examining this famous agape chapter in Scripture.

Divide a journal page with the following two topics: "Love Is" and "Love Isn't." Record all of your findings about love under the appropriate heading. Also notice the powerful verses directly before and after 1 Corinthians 13.

ABIDE

Using your notes, place a check mark by the attributes that you exemplify in a typical day.

I can tell you personally that this chapter always convicts me! No matter how far I've come in living a life of love, I continue to fail. I fall short of consistently showing God's pure agape love.

Here's the staggering news: if God resides in you, then you have the very Source of love *living in you*. Christ is your life! Just live out of the overflowing Love that is already within. Get this—the whole agape love thing is not about you ... but about Him! Allow His loving nature to flow through you. Choose to walk in it. Love is God's holy calling for us.

Do not get discouraged by the process! Understand that He is at work as the Author and Finisher of your faith—and of the faith of your brothers and sisters in Christ, too!

Take a look at this wonderful passage in 1 John:

> How great is the love the Father has lavished on us, that we should be called children of God! And that is what we are! The reason the world does not know us is that it did not know him. Dear friends, now we are children of God, and what we will be has not yet been made known. But we know that when he appears, we shall be like him, for we shall see him as he is. Everyone who has this hope in him purifies himself, just as he is pure. (1 John 3:1-3)

Give up on trying to love in your own strength. Apart from Christ, you cannot truly love. Rest in the power of Christ in you! Don't get down on yourself but simply give up on yourself. Die to your self-efforts and rely on Christ!

I have a favorite verse that I say on a regular basis. It guides my heart and mind to be in alignment with the mind of the Spirit. This is the verse to which I choose to submit: "The only thing that counts is faith expressing itself through love" (Galatians 5:6).

When I become offended or annoyed by someone (usually this is a family member), before reacting in an unloving manner, I mentally rehearse this scripture and yield my heart to God's will.

Just yesterday, I had many opportunities to respond unlovingly toward my family. A trail of dirt from muddy shoes went *all* through the house; a request I gave was ignored; and keeping all of my fun-loving kids quiet during a school lesson was next to impossible. There's more to tell, but you get the point.

I wish I could tell you that in every situation I was gentle in my reproach. Irritability is an ugly thing. But there were some moments of dynamite victory, too. There were occasions when I chose to obey God and express my faith by showing love. I chose to forgive and not to mention the dirty floor and the ignored request. It felt so much better than airing my grievances! The "teaching" lesson can wait for another time.

What Bible verse can you commit to memory today as your reminder to follow the way of love?

Day 5   Love Unifies

SEEK GOD

Don't allow anything to stand in the way of spending some quiet moments with God each day. Give all of your heart, soul, mind, and strength to your loving Father in prayer. Enjoy and delight yourself in Him. Ask God to reveal Himself and His truth as you study today.

OBTAIN TRUTH

Read Romans 13:8-14, Romans 14, and Romans 15:1-7.

Identify the characteristics of love in Romans today by compiling a list again under the headings "Love Is" and "Love Is Not." I recommend that you first read through Chapter 14 without stopping and then recording your findings.

ABIDE

It is vital for the body of Christ to abide in love! Unity, sincere love, and concern for other believers are God's heart and Jesus' prayer in John 17:20-23.

We as the Body of Christ are a beautiful, Spirit-empowered extension of Christ Jesus, who is our Head. We have one Lord, one faith, and one baptism. We are a family!

All around the world, the Family of God is working together to lift the oppressed and to assist, feed, and care for the sick and impoverished. We are intentionally prayerful, sacrificially giving, lovingly serving, powerfully preaching, thoughtfully teaching, and passionately fulfilling the Great Commission. We help to serve the persecuted and the orphans. We create new books, blogs, movies, music, websites, and other tools to equip each other for ministry.

It is absolutely amazing! I am in awe of the work of Christ in His Church. I truly love the Church! I love my Family!

You may hold similar affections. But is our love always sincere? Do we always do what leads to peace? Do we intentionally encourage one another and place each other in higher esteem than ourselves?

We have an unending debt to demonstrate Christ's love!

I have witnessed much pride and self-promotion in Christ's Body. Debates and arguments over methods that are not essential to salvation have divided many. I've witnessed the truth that knowledge puffs up.

Even more upsetting to me is that I have been guilty of doing many of the same things. I have looked down on others who've disagreed with me. I have held grudges and gossiped.

Have you done something similar?

Brothers and sisters, this should not be! It grieves my heart deeply. I know that it grieves our Lord and Savior much more to see His children not getting along. Love builds up! Jesus declared our main role or assignment while living on Earth in John 13.

Jesus proclaimed, "'A new command I give you: Love one another. As I have loved you, so you must love one another. By this all men will know that you are my disciples, if you love one another'" (John 13:34-35).

If there is an area of sin of which the Holy Spirit is convicting you, write it down. Write it all down. Admit your sin to God and turn from it. The grace and mercy of God await you. Healing and restoration await you.

> Therefore confess your sins to each other and pray for each other so that you may be healed. The prayer of a righteous person is powerful and effective. (James 5:16)

The most appropriate way to end our study on love is to abide by the life-giving words of the apostle Paul. He simply instructs, "Do everything in love" (1 Corinthians 16:14),

CRAVE

Pray the following prayer for yourself daily. Commit to praying it for a certain length of time (maybe a week, a month, six months, or a year). We believe that God will change you through this.

> I pray that you, being rooted and established in love, may have power, together with all the Lord's holy people, to grasp how wide and long and high and deep is the love of Christ, and to know this love that surpasses knowledge—that you may be filled to the measure of all the fullness of God. Now to him who is able to do immeasurably more than all we ask or imagine, according to his power that is at work within us, to him be glory in the church and in Christ Jesus throughout all generations, for ever and ever! Amen. (Ephesians 3:17-21)

PART 4

REACH OUT

"The harvest is plentiful, but the workers are few.
Ask the Lord of the harvest, therefore, to send out workers into his field."

(Matthew 9:37)

SOAR Participant,

You made it! You are officially in the final part of SOAR:

Reach Out!

Reach Out is our opportunity to embrace our God-given gifts and take them into a broken world! Are you ready?

We are sure that you have dreams deep in your heart, and our prayer is that those dreams will surface through Reach. We pray that God will grow your confidence and trust in Him to carry out His special calling for you!

We love you so much. We cannot express how much we have enjoyed this journey with you.

We love you!

Amy and Sheri

REACH: Overview

Jesus trained the disciples. He said to them, "The harvest is plentiful, but the workers are few. Ask the Lord of the harvest, therefore, to send out workers into his field" (Matthew 9:37).

Reach is the final part of SOAR. You have been trained and encouraged in the following:

- Seeking to know God more
- Prayer and worship
- Knowing your identity in Jesus Christ
- Listening to the voice of God
- Living in and by the power of God

Now is the time to put to work all of the transformation and revelation that you have obtained through SOAR!

Reach is all about releasing *you* as a laborer for Christ. It's your turn to go boldly into the world to sow truth and harvest souls for the glory of God. Reach will motivate, encourage, and help you to get started!

Maybe you recognize that you do not yet have a relationship with Father God. If you are ready to invite Him into your life, pray the following:

Father, I confess that I have sinned against You. Please forgive me. I ask You to be my Savior. I realize that I could never earn salvation on my own. I put my trust in Jesus. I believe that Jesus took the punishment for my sin on the cross. I believe that You love me and that Jesus died and rose again so that I can be forgiven and know You. Fill me with Your Holy Spirit. I give You my life. Thank you for loving me and giving me new life. I trust that I am Yours and am now sealed with Your Spirit! In Jesus' name, Amen.

Now leave your old life of sin and rebellion—because you have been made new, clean, and holy! This study is a perfect way for you to begin to grow in your understanding of what you now have in Christ Jesus and to renew your mind to become more like Him! Welcome to the family of God!

Our prayer for you is that you will know God more and more every day, that He will flood the eyes of your heart with revelation, and that you will continually surrender your life to Him, moment by moment!

Study Outline

Week 1: Appointed and Anointed – with Amy

Week 2: Armed in Attitude – with Sheri

Week 3: Faithfully Equipped – with Amy

Week 4: Revive the Dream – with Sheri

Week 5: Multiply with Teamwork – with Amy and Sheri

Week 6: Good News – with Amy, Sheri, and Testimonies

REACH OUT - Week One
Appointed and Anointed (with Amy)

Memory Verse:

> "Whoever wants to be first must be slave of all. For even the Son of Man did not come to be served, but to serve, and to give his life as a ransom for many." (Mark 10:44-45)

Video Review: http://www.soarwithgod.com/Reach/Reach.html

The bad news: _____

The good news: _____

> "The Spirit of the Lord is upon Me, Because He has anointed Me To preach the gospel to the poor; He has sent Me to heal the brokenhearted, To proclaim liberty to the captives And recovery of sight to the blind, To set at liberty those who are oppressed." (Luke 4:19 and Isaiah 61)

> Whoever claims to live in him must walk as Jesus did. (1 John 2:6)

> "You did not choose me, but I chose you and appointed you to go and bear fruit— fruit that will last." John 15:16

I am to carry on the King's mission and be a:

Restorer of _____

Repairer of _____

(Isaiah 58:12)

Is Christ living His heart and purposes through me?

One big enemy: _____

I am called to be a _____.

> Therefore, I urge you, brothers, in view of God's mercy, to offer your bodies as living sacrifices, holy and pleasing to God—this is your spiritual act of worship. (Romans 12:1)

When should I reach out?

_____ IT, _____ IT!

Day 1 Live Like Jesus

I have many personal biases, especially when it comes to my children. I want their soccer teams to win their games. I favor their dance performances over those of other children. Why? Because they are my babies! I do care about other kids but not nearly to the degree that I do my own. Do you ever show favoritism? Is this acceptable to God? Can we genuinely serve Christ if we play favorites?

SEEK GOD

Humble yourself before the Holy One. Magnify and worship Him for who He is. Christ is your life. Abandon your life wholly to Him. Be still and experience His presence in prayer.

OBTAIN TRUTH

Read and meditate on the memory verse. Write down this week's memory verse on a note card or in your notebook so that you can work on committing it to memory throughout your week.

Read James 2.

Are you ready to start a new SOAR notebook? I am! Let's get started. Write the following heading in your notebook: "Favoritism and Faith." Read James 2 and record the essential instructions given about these two subjects. For example, "Love your neighbor as yourself." What is God's instruction, and how can you carry it out practically?

ABIDE

Jesus' earthly life was one of loving, sacrificial service. His life was the exact representation, mission, and heart of God the Father. Now this is your mission according to 1 John 2:6: You are to walk as Jesus walked! Let that sink in for a minute. Do you feel the power of this mission that you have been given?

Jesus never showed favoritism. Everyone was a candidate for His compassion, friendship, healing, love, and grace. Jesus was the perfect example of faith in action! His love was never dormant or idle.

Jesus asked a gut-wrenching question in Luke 6:46 when He admonished a crowd of listeners, saying, "'Why do you call me, "Lord, Lord," and do not do what I say?'"

This is how we know what love is: Jesus Christ laid down his life for us. And we ought to lay down our lives for our brothers. If anyone has material possessions and sees his brother in need but has no pity on him, how can the love of God be in him? Dear children, let us not love with words or tongue but with actions and in truth. (1 John 3:16-18)

Ask God to help you hear His promptings when He asks you to reach out.

REACH OUT

Ask the Holy Spirit to show you how to live out what you've just read in His Word.

To whom can you reach out in love this week?

Below, circle those in need who are in your life right now:

Your Spouse – Neighbor – Your Child – Coworker – Poor – Abused – Homeless – Lost (without Christ) – Persecuted – Sick Discouraged – Orphaned – Widowed – Imprisoned – Elderly – Grieving – Discouraged – Addicted – Lonely – Depressed Uneducated Physically – Disabled –Weary – Anxious – Single Parent – Marital Problems – Hurting Teen

What are the needs of your family (spouse, child, parents, siblings, etc.)? _____
_____
_____

What can you do to begin reaching out today? Write down your first action step. If you haven't stepped out before in Christ, one good way to start is to identify the easiest thing that you can accomplish from start to finish. Start there.

Action Step #1:

_____

Day 2   My Father's Business

When Jesus was only twelve years old, His parents found Him in the temple courts of Jerusalem. He asked his worried parents, "Why did you seek me? Did you not know that I must be about my Father's business?" (Luke 2:49).

God has Kingdom work for all of His children. The question that we should all want answered, then, is: What does God want us to do?

We *can* know His will. Thankfully, He shows us the way through His Word!

In Matthew 6:10, Jesus taught His disciples to pray for God's work to be accomplished throughout this earth when He prayed, "Your kingdom come, your will be done on earth as it is in heaven."

Jesus even declared the unthinkable: "I no longer call you servants, because a servant does not know his master's business. Instead, I have called you friends, for everything that I learned from my Father I have made known to you" (John 15:15).

SEEK GOD

Cherish and treasure your Father in prayer today. In view of God's sacrifice for you, wholeheartedly offer your all to Him. He is Worthy!

OBTAIN TRUTH

Remember to review your memory verse.

Read Ephesians 2:10, Romans 12:9-21, and 1 Thessalonians 5:11-24

Take out your notebook and place "My Father's Business" as your heading. As you study today's passages, list your God-given mandates. Respond to the Father's instructions with joyful obedience.

ABIDE

Are you wondering what the Father's will is for your life? This is His will for you: you and I were created to know Him and to do His good works! It's so simple that we can often miss it.

It's simply SOAR. Seek God. Obtain His Truth. Abide in Him. Reach out to others. It's basic, yet profound.

The God-given mandates that you listed are not the typical way of the world. It's weird to be kind to those who hurt you and to love your enemies. Some will think you are foolish. You will probably look like a fool to the masses. But wouldn't you rather be a fool for Christ than a fool without Christ?

Here's a question that we should ask ourselves every day: Do I want to be a "foolish Christian" or a "fool for Christ?"

All throughout the Bible, God gave His children straightforward and specific codes of conduct. And all throughout the Bible we find one tragic example after another of people who rejected God's ways to live life their way.

Be a fool for Christ! To this you were called. A "fool for Christ" will risk it all for the sake of the King. It won't always be easy or make sense, but God will guide you and has equipped you in every way for His Kingdom purposes.

God has often led me to reach out to others in ways that I haven't understood. Like me, you might send a letter, serve the needy, give away resources, or make a friendly phone call, all in faith, believing that God directed you. Sometimes you will have the joy of knowing the beautiful impact that a simple act of love has made. Other times you'll be left wondering, feeling uncertain and a bit foolish because your attempt seemed fruitless. The Father's ways and thoughts are higher and He simply wants us to stay the course of lovingly following His plans. When you leave all of the results up to Him, it takes the pressure and focus off of you.

REACH OUT

After some time of prayer and reflection, write down what you know you are specifically called to live out. Seek God and ask Him to reveal your next step.

Day 3   Love in Word and Deed

You can advance the Kingdom of God one step at a time.

Just love!

Love is never silent even when words are not spoken.
Love is never lazy even in times of rest.
Love is always reaching, stretching forward.
Love is available for every opportunity it is given.
Love is a consuming fire destroying the devil's schemes.
Love is never small. It's always big, always significant.
Small acts of love are the path to big change.

SEEK GOD

Enter prayer with your Father in joyful confidence. Allow yourself ample time to worship the King, make requests, and listen for His guidance.

> Let us then approach the throne of grace with confidence, so that we may receive mercy and find grace to help us in our time of need. (Hebrews 4:16)

OBTAIN TRUTH

Read your memory verse today.

Read Isaiah 58 and 61:1-3.

From today's readings, Isaiah 58 and 61:1-3, write a list of all the Kingdom work that God wants you to pursue. Star those items that make your heart beat with passion or get your imagination spinning with what-ifs.

ABIDE

Do you feel a little overwhelmed by all of the troubles and needs of people in this world? Don't be. God is able! He tells you so in Isaiah 41:10: "So do not fear, for I am with you; do not be dismayed, for I am your God. I will strengthen you and help you; I will uphold you with my righteous right hand."

Whom is God calling you to encourage, strengthen, or train? With whom can you share Jesus Christ? Whom can you nurture? Provide for materially? Rescue? Disciple? Correct? Mentor? Assist? Befriend? Visit? Pray for? Honor? Bless? Hold accountable? Sharpen? Listen to? To whom would God have you offer mercy, grace, and forgiveness?

Has God been whispering to you? Ask Him to direct you to people into whom you can pour your life. Now, simply go forward in faith, trusting that God will be faithful to direct your path.

REACH OUT

Pray. Ask God to direct your heart and mind. Act promptly and obediently to God's convictions and assignments.

Don't wait. Respond to a need today!

If you do not know what your next step is, try one of these ideas:

- Call your church staff and ask if you can help them or someone they know.
- Go online and research the needs of your local community or state.
- Ask around on Twitter or Facebook, or by texting friends or family.

Day 4 Appointed and Anointed

The fact that you are called and set apart by God is pretty special—unfathomable, actually! It's absolutely incredible that God could use the likes of you and me, yet He does. How? Why? Let's look into this wonder of wonders today.

SEEK GOD

Devote yourself to a moment of sincere prayer. Ask God to give you the power to follow Him in all things. Praise Him for times past when He gave you the courage to follow Him!

OBTAIN TRUTH

Don't forget to review your memory verse:

> "Whoever wants to be first must be slave of all. For even the Son of Man did not come to be served, but to serve, and to give his life as a ransom for many." (Mark 10:44-45)

Read Jeremiah 1:4-10.

Examine God's provisions and sovereign plans in the prophet Jeremiah's life in Jeremiah 1:4-10. As you make these observations, use the titles "God's Role" and "Jeremiah's Responsibility" and write down your findings.

ABIDE

Think about who God is for a moment.

God the Father is the Almighty One, the Creator of the Universe. He is

Jesus Christ the Messiah, the Savior of the World, the Redeemer, the Prince of Peace, and the King of kings.

God is the Sovereign Lord and the Source of all Sources. And this same God is *with* you and *for* you.

He appointed you and set you apart for His glorious purposes. I pray that these truths completely blow your mind and that you'll never tire of thinking about them.

Truthfully, though, you won't always feel that you're cut out for fulfilling any glorious purposes of God. You know your weaknesses all too well. Guess what? So does God. But you might be forgetting that your very life is empowered by God. In 2 Corinthians 12:9 the Holy Spirit tells Paul, "My grace is sufficient for you, for my power is made perfect in weakness."

Paul's response in the last part of the verse above should be ours. "Therefore I will boast all the more gladly about my weaknesses, so that Christ's power may rest on me." Why would God work through our weaknesses except to reveal His greatness and glory? If we could do God's will in our own strength, then what glory would God receive? None, of course! However, we have no real strength apart from Him. Thankfully, we are never apart from Him! It is in Him that we live and move and have our very being!

Jeremiah's calling from God wasn't about Jeremiah's ability but, rather, about God's ability. God appoints and anoints you. He is faithful, and he will accomplish His will through you!

REACH OUT

Write out two separate lists. Compile a list of five of your weaknesses and make another one with *just* five of God's strengths. Next, compare your lists!

You are appointed and anointed for this day! Now go reach out in the strength that God provides.

Day 5   Go and Do Likewise

I like comfort. I have a very soft, comfy bed and pillow to sleep on at night. I often realize that many do not have such luxuries, so I am beyond grateful. However, some mornings I find it hard to leave my comfortable bed to face the day's many and certain challenges; but I know I must. We all must, if we want to follow Christ.

Serving Christ will never be on the easy, comfortable, and most traveled road.

SEEK GOD

What are you holding onto? Are you being real and transparent with God in your prayer time? Lay it down before the Father. He is better than a best friend. You can tell Him all things. You can truly lay down all of your burdens—right now. Immerse yourself in passionate prayer with the Father.

OBTAIN TRUTH

Do you have your memory verse down yet? If so, recite it for someone. If not, continue reviewing it.

Read Luke 10:25-37.

Answer the following questions:

- What real or possible sacrifices did the Samaritan make for his neighbor?

- What excuses might the priest and Levite have had for not helping?
- Do you think these excuses were acceptable? Why or why not?

To this you were called, because Christ suffered for you, leaving you an example, that you should follow in his steps. (1 Peter 2:21)

ABIDE

We can be such wimpy Christians. Our spirit desires to reach out in love, but our selfish flesh often interferes and provides us with all kinds of creative excuses to ignore the Holy Spirit's call.

> Anyone, then, who knows the good he ought to do and doesn't do it, sins.
> James 4:17)

We forget that following Christ means carrying a cross. Think a bit about physically carrying an actual cross—a big, heavy, scratchy, wooden one. Ugh. Nope. I do not want to sign up for that job.

Thankfully, literal cross-carrying is not mandatory. Yet consider the cost that remains: following Christ means sacrifice, opposition, and weariness as well as joy, peace, and freedom.

> Therefore, my dear brothers, stand firm. Let nothing move you. Always give
> yourselves fully to the work of the Lord, because you know that your labor in the
> Lord is not in vain.
> (1 Corinthians 15:58)

J. Oswald Sanders told the story of a native missionary who walked barefoot from village to village, preaching the gospel in India. After a long day of many miles and great discouragement, he came to a certain village and tried to share the Gospel but was driven out of town and rejected. So he went to the edge of the village and lay down under a tree; and he slept from exhaustion.

When he awoke, people were hovering over him, and the whole town was gathered around to hear him speak. The village headman explained that they had come to look him over while he was sleeping. When they saw his blistered feet, they concluded that he must be worthy to listen to, and that they had been wrong to reject him. They wanted to hear the message for which he was willing to suffer so greatly.

Has reaching out to someone ever caused you to have to endure some suffering? If so, did this tempt you to give up, or did it compel you forward?

How beautiful on the mountains are the feet of those who bring good news, who proclaim peace, who bring good tidings, who proclaim salvation who say to Zion, "Your God reigns!" (Isaiah 52:7)

If someone forces you to go one mile, go with him two miles. Give to the one who asks you, and do not turn away from the one who wants to borrow from you. (Matthew 5:41-42)

Let us not become weary in doing good, for at the proper time we will reap a harvest if we do not give up. Therefore, as we have opportunity, let us do good to all people, especially to those who belong to the family of believers. (Galatians 6:9-10)

REACH OUT

Pray and ask God to reveal to you a way to go the extra mile for someone today. Ask God to give you the strength to be a fool for Him. Ask God to help you go and live as Jesus did!

Expect God to direct your thoughts in this decision.

Write down what God is leading you to do. Now go! Reach out! God will give you the strength and love through the Holy Spirit to carry it out.

CRAVE

Read Matthew 25:14-46. The small things we do, matter. What are some small ways in which you can live faithfully for God? Write down at least three ideas.

REACH OUT – Week Two
Armed in Attitude (with Sheri)

Memory Verses:

Be imitators of God, therefore, as dearly loved children. (Ephesians 5:1)
"Father, if you are willing, take this cup from me; yet not my will, but yours be done."
(Luke 22:42)

To have the attitude of Christ, you must know that you are qualified— not by your training or skill, but by the *One Qualifier*, the Holy Spirit. You are qualified! Having the attitude of Christ means that you will be interrupted. The attitude of Christ knows this: you are an alien with a new purpose and mission to take back territory for the Kingdom of God. The attitude of Christ is laying down your will and taking up the will of God—no matter the cost.

Video Review: http://www.soarwithgod.com/Reach/Reach.html

For he chose us in him before the creation of the world to be holy and blameless in his sight. (Ephesians 1:4)

But you will receive power when the Holy Spirit comes on you; and you will be my witnesses (Acts 1:8)

Be imitators of God, therefore, as dearly loved children and live a life of love, just as Christ loved us and gave himself up for us as a fragrant offering and sacrifice to God. (Ephesians 5:1-2)

Attitude of acquisition – to be on a mission to possess or acquire

Christ had the ultimate _____!

For God so loved the world that he gave his one and only Son, that whoever believes in him shall not perish but have eternal life. (John 3:16)

Father, if you are willing, take this cup from me; yet not my will, but yours be done. (Luke 22:42)

Attitude of acquisition – to be on a mission to possess or acquire _____.

Jesus' Attitude Lived Out

1.   _____   _____

2.   Reach Out –   _____   _____   _____   _____

3.   _____ Interruptions

4.   _____ Lives

I take up Christ's attitude of acquisition.

I know I'm qualified, not by training or skill, but by the Holy Spirit.

I am a connector between God and the lost. I expect to be interrupted. In fact, I schedule time for interruptions.

I am an alien to this world. Everywhere I go, I am on a mission to take back territory for the Kingdom of God.

I lay down my will, my agenda, and my life to take up the will of God no matter the cost to me—in Jesus' name!

Day 1   Choosing His Agenda

Wouldn't you have loved to be one of the twelve disciples? Imagine what it would have been like to experience Christ in day-to-day life and to be directly trained by Him!

The disciples gave up everything to follow Jesus. They served alongside Him and performed miracles by His name, yet they were still shocked, amazed, and doubtful when they saw His awesome works. Without the Holy Spirit, they couldn't really know Him (Read John 16:12-13).

SEEK GOD

Seek God through prayer first thing in your day. Find a quiet place so that you can not only pray but also listen.

OBTAIN TRUTH

You have two memory verses this week. They are both amazing, and if you place them deep within your heart, you will remember them at the perfect times.

Today's reading:
Luke 5:1-11, Matthew 4:18-22, Matthew 26:47-56, John 21:1-14

In your notebook, write down everything you learn from reading about the life of the disciples before, during, and after Jesus' ministry.

Old habits and traditions are hard to change. It's easy to migrate back to your old way of doing things. Do you think that the disciples ever felt abandoned or failed by Jesus? Do you think that they forgot Jesus' last words to them? They drifted back to their old training and their old lifestyle before Jesus— fishing.

Can you relate to the disciples in this? If so, how?

ABIDE

In John 10:17-18 Jesus said, "The reason my Father loves me is that I lay down my life—only to take it up again. No one takes it from me, but I lay it down of my own accord. I have authority to lay it down and authority to take it up again. This command I received from my Father."

Jesus had authority over His own life. Jesus could have followed His own agenda, if He had so desired, or He could lay it down. Thankfully, for you and me, He laid it down!

You have this same right. You can take up your own agenda to do life your way, or you can lay it down to pick up the agenda of God.

Which will you do? This is not a one-time decision; it's a daily choice.

REACH OUT

What agenda(s) do you need to lay down to make room for God's agenda in your daily life?

I was on pace to become partner in one of the world's largest accounting firms. Then one day I realized that I needed to lay down my career and drive for success to be a stay-at-home mom and minister.

What is it for you? Most likely, you know exactly what it is. You may be feeling convicted by the Holy Spirit right now. Just start by writing it down. Ask God to reveal your hidden, and obvious, self-appointed agendas. Now ask Him to help you lay them down.

Day 2   You Are Qualified

When I graduated from college, I thought that I was a big shot. I had my accounting degree, and I was ready to take on some important job. It wasn't long until I discovered that all my college training hadn't prepared me for my "big time" job. I had no idea what I was doing! It was as if my training started all over again. It wasn't until I started using what I had learned that everything I knew started to gain some value.

SEEK GOD

Pray. Seek God. Ask Him to help you know Him better. Then listen. He will reveal Himself to you more and more—if you just ask and listen.

OBTAIN TRUTH

Review this week's memory verses.

Read Acts 1:8, 2:14-41, Acts 4, Acts 5:12-16, Acts 8:4-8, Acts 9:32-43, and Acts 13:42-52.

According to Acts 1:8, what qualified the disciples to witness and reach out?

From today's verses, write down answers to the following:

- What did the disciples do once they were qualified?
- How did other people view the disciples and the works that they did after they were qualified?

Compare your notes from Day 1 with today's notes. How were the disciples different after they were truly qualified (Acts 1:8)?

What qualifies you to reach out in the name of Jesus Christ?

_____

Do you believe that you are qualified? Why or why not?

_____

_____

_____

ABIDE

If you still do not believe you are qualified, then it could be due to one of two reasons:

1) You don't have a personal relationship with Jesus.

   No problem! God is calling you, or else you wouldn't be here right now. He has been pursuing you for a long time. Just believe and receive His life in exchange for yours today. Confess openly to God that you need a Savior and believe that He took your place on the cross. Give Him your life today.

2) You do not know what you have.

   I once had a hundred dollars hidden away. I totally forgot about it until I found it ten years later (gasp)! I couldn't use what I didn't know, or remember, that I had. Maybe this describes you.

Ephesians 1:19-20 says that you have the same power that raised Christ from the dead. You may not know what you have.

If you aren't sure what you have been given through Christ, return to the Abide section of SOAR (Week Four) for a refresher.

REACH OUT

You are empowered and qualified by God Himself! Share your salvation testimony with one person today or tomorrow. Set a goal to share your story more often. Can you make a commitment to share it once a month, once a week, once a day, or more? Revelation 12:11 reads, "They overcame him (the evil one) by the blood of the Lamb and by the word of their testimony."

Your story will change someone's life ... if you share it.

Ask God with whom you should share your story. Listen. Pay attention and seize the opportunity when it presents itself.

Day 3   Pit-Stop Attitude

SEEK GOD

What's burdening you today? Do you have a transparent prayer relationship with God? He knows your thoughts before you ever speak them (Psalm 139). Talk openly to God. Lay down your burdens and any condemnation at His feet. Don't rise up from prayer time until you are refreshed.

OBTAIN TRUTH

Don't forget to review this week's awesome memory verses! Are there other verses that you want to remember? If so, write them down.

Read John 4:1-42. Label two new pages in your notebook: "Samaritan Woman" and "Jesus."

Answer the following questions:

Samaritan Woman

- What was she like before her encounter with Jesus?
- How was she changed by this encounter with Jesus?
- What influence and reputation do you think this woman had in her community before she went to the well that day?
- What impact do you think she had in Samaria after she went to the well?

Jesus

In this encounter with the Samaritan woman, it was as if Jesus were on a road trip. He stopped in at the gas station for a soda, yet he ended up postponing His trip for two days because of what happened at this pit stop!

- Why did Jesus talk to this woman?
- How did Jesus make her feel?
- What was His true purpose at the well?
- Just for fun: Do you think He ever quenched His thirst with a drink of that yummy wellwater?

If you were on a road trip, would you be aware enough of others at a pit stop to recognize a need?

Your light could transform a person at a pit stop, but would you be willing to divert your plans for a day or two if it meant that you could minister to a whole town? What do you think might prohibit you from doing so?

ABIDE

Abiding in the Spirit is a moment-by-moment, step-by-step decision. It's the life that continually surrenders each moment to the will of God rather than to your own to-do list. Jesus was trying to get somewhere, but having the attitude of Christ isn't a destination. It's a journey.

REACH OUT

This week, make time for pit stops. Maybe you need to give up something that has kept you from having any margin in your life.

When we have the attitude of Christ, we'll willingly accept divinely scheduled interruptions because we know that our schedule is not our own. However, I want you to reframe this thought to:

Schedule Your Interruptions!

In your daily calendar, schedule time for interruptions. With the attitude of Christ, we will be interrupted. Instead of being caught off guard, schedule it!

Arrive places early so that you can be interrupted. Plan to leave late so that you can see a need and fill it. Go to work and start your day looking for needs rather than jumping straight into the pile of papers on your desk. When you go out, look for someone to encourage, share Christ with, and pray with. Don't give yourself thirty minutes to do a one-hour job and then be in a rush so that you miss the moment to reach out!

If you are not sure how to reach out, or to whom, look up the following verses: Matthew 5:43-48, James 1:27, 1 Timothy 5:3-16, Acts 4:32-35, 1 Thessalonians 5:11-15, and Hebrews 3:13.

Day 4   Attitude of Acquisition

When I was a kid, a lot of people talked about UFOs. I thought that aliens could be super-powered beings that might come to take over the earth.

May I remind you of something? You *are* an alien! You belong to another Homeland and have been armed with the power and authority of God.

1 Peter 2:11 says, "Dear friends, I urge you, as aliens and strangers in the world, to abstain from sinful desires, which war against your soul."

SEEK GOD

Pray to your God today. Ask Him what it means to be His alien. Ask Him to open your eyes to all that you possess in Him.

OBTAIN TRUTH

Review the memory verses.

Read Genesis 17:8 and Mark 16:13-19. From these verses, write down what Christians should be doing with their time.

We are aliens to this world. Accorindg to Genesis 17:8, God told Abraham that He would give him all of the land where he was a stranger. God gave Abraham an attitude of acquisition.

Jesus had an attitude of acquisition. Let's define these two words:

- Attitude means a way of thinking or feeling, reflected in a person's behavior.
- Acquire means to buy or obtain an asset for oneself.

Because God loved you so much (John 3:16), Jesus' attitude was reflected in His behavior. He came to this earth to acquire your freedom and to reconcile you to Himself.

Do you have this kind of attitude? Ephesians 5:1 says, "Be imitators of God, therefore, as dearly loved children." Pray for your attitude—to be an imitation of God.

Jesus gave us this command in Mark 16:15: "He said to them, 'Go into all the world and preach the good news to all creation.'"

You and I have an attitude of acquisition for *something*. But God has not given you the same power that raised Christ from the dead simply to acquire your next flatscreen television. Are your thoughts and attitudes in line with God's?

ABIDE

You are an alien now. An alien listens to "mission control." You should no longer be in control, but you must surrender to *your* mission control—God. Aliens should have Christ's attitude of acquisition.

Read the following poem aloud. Post it and share it with others.

I take up the attitude of acquisition and surrender to the will of God.

In Christ, I'm an alien to this Earth.

Through Him I have had the new birth.

I will celebrate the pit stops in my life.

I will serve those in need, feed the hungry, and resolve strife.

In scheduled interruptions, I will make Christ known.

Future generations will know God is on the throne.

Yes, I take up the attitude of acquisition and surrender to the will of God.

REACH OUT

What territory has God given you to acquire? What hearts are lost among your family, friends, and co-workers? People need what you have.

What corner of your world can you possess in order to share God's love, His forgiveness, His prosperity, His peace, His healing, and His freedom?

Make a list of all the people you know who don't know Christ.

Put them in order of those who may be most likely to accept the goodness of Jesus to those least likely. Ask Father God for wisdom in this. Start down the list and share Jesus with them until you are finished.

Have the attitude of acquisition with your immediate family, then with your neighbors and everywhere you go—restaurants, the grocery store, work, the airport, or sports events—anywhere you are.

Are you willing to lay down your life in order to be an alien in Christ, no matter the cost?

There are countries where you could be imprisoned or killed if you live outwardly as God's alien. In the United States, where I live, we are still free to live as aliens. If you and I can't live boldly in a free country, how could our faith possibly uphold in times of true persecution?

If you want to see sold-out aliens in action who are facing persecution, check out http://www.persecution.com/.

Go! Reach! Be God's alien and take possession of lost souls in your land—in the stores, in your college, in your office, and every place you go!

Day 5   God's Laborers

SEEK GOD

Ask Father to give you an attitude of acquisition and action steps to go along with it. God wants to use you. Ask Him to make you usable. Tell Him what's on your heart. He always wants to hear from you.

OBTAIN TRUTH

Don't forget about the memory verses this week.

Read Luke 22:42, Matthew 9:37, John 14:12, Mark 16:17-18, and

1 Timothy 2:3-4.

From today's Bible reading, write down the answer to this question: What does God want to accomplish through you, Alien?

ABIDE

Jesus had the ultimate attitude of acquisition! He paid the price of His life in exchange for yours. He anguished in His soul before going to the cross, yet He knew what He had to do. He surrendered to the will of God.

> "Father, if you are willing, take this cup from me; yet not my will, but yours be done." (Luke 22:42)

He did it for you. He did it for me. He did it for your enemies. He did it for the friend you may never have forgiven. He did it for all humanity so that they could have the opportunity to know Him personally.

> This is good, and pleases God our Savior, who wants all men to be saved and to come to a knowledge of the truth. (1 Timothy 2:3-4)

Since Christ did all this, what right do we have to think we can place our agenda higher than God's?

Living in the attitude of Christ is not an easy task. Jesus himself sweat drops of blood.

It is hard work. It's hard to lay down your busy agenda. You may have to give up something you treasure in order to help someone else. For example, one of our friends recently gave up his own kidney to an old high-school friend who needed a transplant.

Living this way may seem too much to ask, but there are rewards in laying down your life and picking up the attitude of Christ:

- You will get to see the greater works of God!
  I tell you the truth, anyone who has faith in me will do what I have been doing. He will do even greater things than these, because I am going to the Father. (John 14:12)

- You will receive eternal rewards in heaven!
  His work will be shown for what it is, because the Day will bring it to light. It will be revealed with fire, and the fire will test the quality of each man's work. If what he has built survives, he will receive his reward. If it is burned up, he will suffer loss; he himself will be saved, but only as one escaping through the flames. (1 Corinthians 3:13-15)

REACH OUT

Understanding that you are an alien *will* transform you into a laborer. Jesus said that there was a harvest ready; but there are not enough laborers to bring in the harvest.

Have you ever had a garden? When the produce is ripe, if it's not harvested, it spoils.

I wonder if that could happen with people. If they are ready to receive Christ and we don't give them the good news, do they lose their opportunity? I'm not sure. What I do know is that I do not want that happening on my watch!

We've been given a mighty, wonderful gift, and we should reach out according to God's will, not ours. Are you with me?

After *seeking God*, what do you believe God wants to do in and through you?

_____

_____

_____

Make this your confession. Write it down and place it on your mirror.

Before I leave the house today, I will adjust my attitude; in Christ I'll stay. Every door I enter, I will look for the lost and seize the opportunity to share in His cross.

CRAVE

Are you really hungry to know how God has qualified you to share His light among men?

Read the book of Acts.

Make a list of the bold behaviors of the disciples throughout Acts. How did others perceive them? How were lives changed? I pray that this motivates you: "Be imitators of God, therefore, as dearly loved children" (Ephesians 5:1).

REACH OUT – Week Three
Faithfully Equipped (with Amy)

Memory Verse:

> His divine power has given us everything we need for life and godliness through our knowledge of him who called us by his own glory and goodness. (2 Peter 1:3)

Video Review: http://www.soarwithgod.com/Reach/Reach.html

> Each one should use whatever gift he has received to serve others, faithfully administering God's grace in its various forms. (1 Peter 4:10)

1. God has given you _____.

2. The gifts are for _____ others.

3. God wants _____ of the gifts He gives.

Do you know what gifts you've been given?

Do you know how you are called to use your gifts?

God faithfully _____!

Three faithful ways of God in the lives of three men:

1. Gideon: God is faithful to _____!

2. Moses: God is faithful to _____!

3. Jonah: God is faithful to _____!

Have you ever wanted a different gift and calling?

Jesus + You + Me = _____!

> If anyone speaks, he should do it as one speaking the very words of God. If anyone serves, he should do it with the strength God provides, so that in all things God may be praised through Jesus Christ. To him be the glory and the power for ever and ever. Amen. (1 Peter 4:11)

Day 1   Indispensible

You are equipped with gifts and a unique purpose in the body of Christ. God has prepared a role especially for you to carry out. You are needed. You are *indispensible* (Read 1 Corinthians 12:22)!

SEEK GOD

In your time of prayer, ask God for greater depth of insight to know Him more fully.

OBTAIN TRUTH

Read your memory verse aloud twice. Consider writing it down on a notecard so that you can work on it throughout your week.

Read 1 Corinthians 12.

Create a two-column list with the headings, "God Provides" and "The Body." As you read in 1 Corinthians, record the key information about God and His body. You will discover how God planned for His Church, the body, to function together in unity for His glory.

ABIDE

Teaching and mercy are two of my dominant gifts. I love to study the Word and tell whoever will listen about its greatness and meaning. I'm also thrilled when I can respond to others' needs with compassion and serve them.

However, I have always longed for the gift of encouragement, or what some call "exhortation." Encouragers are some of the most enjoyable people to be around. They make you feel great about yourself!

Shouldn't we all try to become better encouragers? In Hebrews 3:13 we are actually instructed to build each other up through encouragement.

Years ago, I began praying and asking God for this gift. I also started to practice using my words to build others up. It was quite awkward at first. Although I'm still not characterized by this gift, over time I have actually become a better exhorter.

However, comparing my gifts with others' takes the focus off of God and places it on me. And I do *not* want to live this way. I still eagerly desire all of the gifts, but in the meantime, I *choose* to embrace, and serve in, the various ways for which He has uniquely called and equipped me.

God had specific plans in mind for you when he chose you to be on His team. He knows exactly how you fit into His Design.

Learn to embrace your God-given gifts and roles. After all, God is a genius! All the parts of His body are absolutely necessary. His body is designed for breathtaking, world-shaking greatness!

Jesus + you + me = Wow!

REACH OUT

Have you identified your God-given spiritual gifts? Go online to www.spiritualgiftstest.com to identify your gifts. It's fast and free! It's an easy and effective way to affirm what God has already placed in you.

Day 2   Fully Assured

There is no need for insecurity and worry when you know that God has called you to a certain task. God is with you! But wait: Are you really sure that it is God guiding you? How can you *truly* know? Today we will look at a similar struggle in the life of Gideon.

SEEK GOD

Enter the throne room of grace and sit with your Mighty Father. Surrender all of your fears and insecurities to Him.

OBTAIN TRUTH

Read your memory verse aloud twice.

Read Judges 6 and 7. As you read the story of Gideon in Judges, take notes. Record God's words and how He helped Gideon to overcome his insecurities.

Now answer the following questions:

- Why do you think Gideon was so uncertain of God's presence with him?
- How many times did God provide Gideon assurance? By what means?
- What are some ways in which Gideon eventually displayed his confidence in God?

ABIDE

Okay, so, I think Gideon and I may be twins (or a least distant cousins). I can easily relate to his lack of confidence and need for repeated reassurance. Can you? Even when God has made Himself and His call quite obvious to me, for days or even weeks later, I'm *still* asking Him for more confirmation. Yes, I've laid out my share of fleeces—strange fleeces too. This was insecurity and perhaps immaturity on my part.

God desires our relationship with Him to be strong so that when He speaks we know it's Him. Then our faith can immediately and unhesitatingly move into action.

Why do you think Gideon was unsure of God's strategy and provision?

Your past experiences do not determine your future successes in Christ.

God is always at work in and behind the scenes. When God says that it's time to act, it's time to act. But you serve a patient and generous God! Praise the Lord that even in your lack of confidence, He's willing to supply what you need to move forward in confidence.

REACH OUT

Are you struggling with insecurities and doubts concerning something that you believe God is leading you to do?

In your notebook, write out your concerns in a prayer to God.

Next, list any and everything that you need in order to take your very next step of obedience confidently.

Ask God to meet you at your point of need(s).

Now wait expectantly as He shows Himself faithful.

Day 3   Fully Empowered

You have everything you need for life and godliness. God is with you. Listen for Him to whisper, "I Am." You've been supplied with the Great I Am as your Help and Strength. If God is for you, then who can be against you?

SEEK GOD

Come before the Father completely humble and eager for His life to be manifested through you. Seek Him. As you do He will increase and you must decrease. (John 3:30)

OBTAIN TRUTH

You'll want to have this week's memory verse hidden in your heart. When you hit a roadblock or feel discouraged, this verse could renew your hope. Meditate on it. It's powerful.

Read Exodus 3 and 4.

From today's reading, write down your answers to the following questions:

- What were all of Moses' doubts concerning God's instructions?
- What were God's reactions and solutions to Moses' issues?

ABIDE

I love power: electric lights, refrigeration, central heat and air, battery-powered laptop computers, cell phones, and fuel-powered automobiles and airplanes! Sheer blessings from above!

These "powers" have made my life more global-minded, informed, timely, connected, and comfortable. I've learned to rely on them every day. Life comes to a near standstill when a power-outage hits our home. It's frustrating and awkward to be without power.

Do you ever feel powerless? Sure. We *all* have.

It can seem awkward and bad when we feel incapable or out of control. This shouldn't be. The truth that God is in control and that we are filled with His power and might is deeply ingrained in us, right? Or is it?

I am called to teach. Yet sometimes I question my ability to write a message and present it. Why?

I am called to parenthood. However, at times I wonder if Craig and I can decide rightly for our children. Why?

I am called to lead. But I sometimes doubt whether or not I can become a better leader for God's church. Why? I am called. Why is that not enough?

Do you feel inadequate? Does this cause you to obey God's calling in your life unwillingly or hesitantly? If so, you are looking at yourself instead of at the one and only "I Am."

So you don't have what it takes? Listen up: No one has what it takes! Only through God can we live, move, and have our being. God is your Almighty Power Source. He never runs low, goes out, or short-circuits! He supplies every ability and gift that you need to fulfill His will.

> Praise the Father, that we can do *all* things through Christ who is our strength!
> (Philippians 4:13)

REACH OUT

Write out any role for which you feel inadequate and try to explain why.

Take the time to process this thoroughly. In all of your weaknesses, the Father wants to empower you with His strength. Acknowledge your need and then depend on Him. Stop looking at yourself and focus on Him.

How will you rely on God's power today? Write down one or two specific answers.

Day 4   Fully Equipped

As you study the book of Jonah, I pray that God will overwhelm you with the realization and magnitude of His great faithfulness. He is the supplier of *all* that you need: the gifts, power, encouragement, time, provision, grace, guidance, and even compassion.

> And my God will meet all your needs according to his glorious riches in Christ Jesus. (Philippians 4:19)

SEEK GOD

Give all of your attention to prayer with your Father. Devote yourself completely to Him. Listen for His guidance.

OBTAIN TRUTH

Read your memory verse aloud a few times. Is it sticking yet? Share it with someone today. It's sure to encourage them.

Read the book of Jonah. (It's only four short chapters.)

While you read, take notes concerning the attitude of Jonah and the character of God:

- What was Jonah's overall attitude toward the people of Nineveh?
- What do you think he needed to change about his attitude? Why?
- In what ways did God provide for Jonah? For Nineveh?

ABIDE

Several times as a young teen, my parents "forced me" to go with them on Lay Renewal ministry trips. For those who don't know what a Lay Renewal is, it's when a group of ministry-minded church members (hence the word "lay," meaning non-pastor) are invited to minister for an entire weekend at another church.

Well, the very idea of spending my treasured weekend with a bunch a people whom I didn't know and doing things that I didn't want to do was just too much to ask. But being under my parents' leadership, what choice did I have? So I always went. Needless to say, my attitude was always stinky. I wasn't concerned about the spiritual condition of people at other churches—at least not enough to want to do anything about it.

I love the statement, "Obedience brings understanding." It's absolutely true. Each time I complied and went on a renewal weekend with my parents, my heart softened and my attitude changed. These experiences taught me about the heart of God, the hearts of His people, and the beauty of Christian church ministries. I was always blessed beyond measure. It's emotional for me now just to remember it.

Like Jonah, I needed to have the Father's heart. I needed to have compassion. Jonah and I were both reluctant to follow God's call because we didn't genuinely care for God's people. You see, even though Nineveh was filled with evil deeds beyond description, God cared for them. He loved them enough to warn them to repent. The same was true for you and me.

> You see, at just the right time, when we were still powerless, Christ died for the ungodly. (Romans 5:6)

Jesus is your Leader! Don't try to run and hide if He guides you to reach out to your enemy or a group of people you've never even noticed before. Be aware, willing, and ready to follow His lead, even if it takes you down a path that is far from your expectations and ideals. As you go, your obedience will bring understanding.

A burdened heart does *not* always precede a calling from God. God will provide you with His heart as you follow Him in obedience.

REACH OUT

Let's dig deep to overcome some hurdles that may keep you from reaching out.

Are you willing to reach out to *anyone*? Have you ever prayed for or ministered to an enemy? If not, are you willing to? Maybe it could be someone who hurt you, offended you, or let you down. Or perhaps it could be someone who was out of your normal safe circle—perhaps an offender, a predator, or a prostitute; or maybe an annoying person, an abuser, or a persecutor?

Would you really minister to them? Would you show them mercy, hope, love, and encouragement, or would you turn your back and run from them?

Is there a part of town that you avoid because of the reputation of the people there? Have you had a judgmental attitude toward people who are different than you: A different race? Culture? Appearance? Income level? Religion? Denomination?

God saved you out of your sin and darkness, so isn't His grace immense enough for everyone else? Maybe God wants to use you to reach the very people you've judged.

If you have had this unholy attitude toward others, stop right now. Repent. Ask God to give you His heart for all people.

A burdened heart does *not* always precede a calling from God.

Ask God to show you, clearly, an unlikely person or group to whom He wants you to reach out, or for whom He wants you to commit to pray. For example, God led me to commit to pray for persecutors of Christians, communist government leaders, and sexual predators.

Day 5   For God's Glory

I'm not good. You're not good. We're not good. *God* is Good!

Christian ministry, missions, serving, and giving are all about healing the world and strengthening the Church for the glory and praise of our good God.

SEEK GOD

Worship God in prayer for who He is. Don't rush this time. Seek to bless the Lord with your genuine pursuit to bring Him the praise He is due. Ask Father to reveal more of Himself to you.

OBTAIN TRUTH

Read your memory verse aloud twice more. Rejoice in this truth.

Read 2 Corinthians 4. As you read, carefully observe each mention of God. In your notebook, take notes under the heading, "Ministry is all about..."

ABIDE

An argument started among the disciples as to which of them would be the greatest. Jesus, knowing their thoughts, took a little child and had him stand beside him. Then he corrected them, "Whoever welcomes this little child in my name welcomes me; and whoever welcomes me welcomes the one who sent me. For he who is least among you all—he is the greatest" (Luke 9:46-48).

Can you believe the disciples argued about this—about who was the greatest? Well, at least these men weren't hypocrites pretending to be humble. Jesus said that the greatest is the least among us. How fascinating and backwards from the world's perspective!

History is filled with the power struggles of man trying to climb to the top. But ultimately, Jesus is the greatest! Therefore we should always pursue making His name known and not our own.

Examine the following verses and notice the common theme:

> Each one should use whatever gift he has received to serve others, faithfully administering God's grace in its various forms. If anyone speaks, he should do it as one speaking the very words of God. If anyone serves, he should do it with the strength God provides, so that in all things God may be praised through Jesus Christ. To him be the glory and the power for ever and ever. Amen. (1 Peter 4:10-11)

> So whether you eat or drink or whatever you do, do it all for the glory of God. (1 Corinthians 10:31)

> And whatever you do, whether in word or deed, do it all in the name of the Lord Jesus, giving thanks to God the Father through him. (Colossians 3:17)

Let's knock out pride! The good deeds that you do for other people, for the Church, and for the Lord are not about you. Our gifts and abilities are given to heal the world, serve and strengthen the Church, and reflect the King's glory.

What you do is not about you but about the building up of God's church. Simply put, your gifts are for giving. It's imperative that you and I not only understand this but also that we live it out daily.

REACH OUT

Have you been wrongly motivated to serve in order to gain attention for yourself?

Father God gave me these words. I believe He wants you to hear Him speak these words to you. Listen closely:

> *Come, draw near and follow Me. I want your whole heart, not just part of it. I want your full devotion now instead of yesterday's leftover sentiments. I will never leave you or forsake you. Turn your heart fully to Me alone. All other love and fondness pales in comparison to knowing and loving Me. My love for you is endless and began before I laid the foundations of My earth. There is nothing I desire more than your heart. Whatever you may do in My name should merely be an overflow from our relationship. I will guide you. You can trust Me. I am faithful. Faithful and True is My name. Look to Me in all things.*

Depend on Me, and I will lead you on the paths that you must take. Because I love you, you need not be afraid. Your strength is in Me. Without Me, you are weak and vulnerable, blind and unstable. But with Me, you have everything that you need.

Spend time in prayer.

REACH OUT – Week Four
Revive the Dream (with Sheri)

Memory Verse:

> Now to him who is able to do immeasurably more than all we ask or imagine, according to his power that is at work within us. (Ephesians 3:20)

Video Review: http://www.soarwithgod.com/Reach/Reach.html

> Now to him who is able to do immeasurably more than all we ask or imagine, according to his power that is at work within us.
> (Ephesians 3:20)

Imagination – mental images; concepts that are not perceived through the senses.

> Now faith is being sure of what we hope for and certain of what we do not see.
> (Hebrews 11:1)

Your imagination will take you somewhere:

THE WILDERNESS or THE PROMISED LAND

How are you in the wilderness?

_____

> Because that, when they knew God, they glorified him not as God, neither were thankful; but became vain in their imaginations, and their foolish heart was darkened. (Romans 1:21 KJV)

How to climb out of the wilderness:

- _____God!
- _____God.
- _____thoughts and imaginations that agree with Truth.

Casting down imaginations, and every high thing that exalteth itself against the knowledge of God, and bringing into captivity every thought to the obedience of Christ. (2 Corinthians 10:5 KJV)

Surrender your thoughts, imagination, and dreams to God.

Remember God's Works: *Write it! Stick it! Read it!*

Revive Your Dreams: *Share it! Stick it! Sort it! Step it! Share it!*

Some versions of this week's memory verse (Ephesians 3:20) say, "to him who is able to do immeasurably more than all we think, ask, imagine or dream." Dreaming or imagining is the process of forming mental images of what is not actually present.

God is able to do more than you can think, ask, imagine, or dream. But what are you thinking, dreaming, and imagining? When I was a little girl, I had a vivid imagination: I dreamed of being a singer, dancer, writer, and actress.

But as a child I suppressed my dreams because people told me that I could never do those things. I eventually gave up on my dreams

Has the fire of your dreams been extinguished as mine was?

God wants His children to dream and imagine again so that He can use us fully to fulfill His purposes on this earth!

By the end of this week, I pray you'll be asking, thinking, imagining, and dreaming from the very heart of God again!

Where do you see yourself within one of the following three categories?

1. *Dream killer* – A dream killer's response to a dream is "can't," "shouldn't," "no," or "never." Such a person fears failure more than he or she knows and fears God. Dream killers' faith is in what they see, which reflects how little they trust God.

2. *Dreamer* – Dreamers dream big dreams but get little accomplished. They see themselves accomplishing great things but still fear failure at their core. They trust God in the things that they know for sure will not result in failure.

3. *Dream lifter* – Dream lifters recognize the full power of the cross. They intentionally stay outside of their comfort zone because they trust in God. They encourage others into action with their excitement and hope for life in Christ!

Which are you—a dreamer, a dream killer, or a dream lifter? Commit this week to seeking God and obtaining His truth. Listen to God, and by the end of this week, I pray, you will be a dream lifter!

Day 1   Uncovering

SEEK GOD

Pray and seek God about this week's memory verse. Ask the Holy Spirit to reveal to you what this verse means and to uncover the dreams that He has placed inside your heart.

OBTAIN TRUTH

Read Jeremiah 29:11-13, Matthew 7:7-8, Romans 12:1-2, and Matthew 25:14-30.

In your notebook write the headings, "What I should do?" and "What God will do." Write down your findings.

What do these verses mean to you as you seek to uncover your dreams?

ABIDE

Is something suppressing your ability to dream? If so, what is it? There are many things that can suppress dreams, including fear, failure, devastation, defeat—or even just the prospect of such things.

In Exodus 14:10-12 we see the Israelites as a good example of what not to do. They let their fear of failure and defeat distract them from their dream of God's promised land.

Fear can cause us to return to our comfort zones. It can cause us to settle for less than God's best.

We have all been there. It can be scary to climb out of our ruts, but it's the best place to be. It puts us right into God's hands. He intended it to be this way.

Consider these thoughts on the parable of the talents, then add to your notes in the Obtain Truth section:

The one-talent investor is a dream killer. He doesn't know God; therefore, he doesn't trust God. He knows what he had heard, and this makes him fear God's wrath. His interest is in protecting himself from harm.

Because he is selfish, this dream killer also avoids doing the hard work of investing. His imagination is focused on the worst possible outcome. God knows his heart and his potential. God is not surprised by the outcome.

The two-talent investor is a dreamer. He pursues endeavors in which he can only succeed. Those successes inflate him with pride in what he delivers to God. However, he really doesn't know God. He only attempts what he's confident he can accomplish. He refuses to live by faith.

His actions overflow out of what he knows, understands, and comprehends. God still rewards his tiny faith, but the investor is oblivious to the fact that his self-preserving mindset limits his opportunity to serve the master.

The five-talent investor is a dream lifter. He knows and trusts God. He risks everything to serve the master. He would rather risk everything for his master than be concerned with himself. His past experience with serving God has proven successful. His hope carries his imagination. His hard work isn't even a consideration or concern.

REACH OUT

Remember the category in which you placed yourself—dreamer, dream killer, or dream lifter. Release past failures, fears, and despair. Give it all to God. Today.

Are you dreaming big dreams without any action? Ask God to reveal where you might not fully know His love and power in your life. Ask others around you to help you identify blind spots where you might not trust God.

If you trust God and are executing on your dreams even in small ways ... celebrate! Whether you have accomplished tangible results is not important. Faith is built by trusting God and taking action without fear of failure.

Day 2   Power by Faith

The second part of this week's verse is important: "...*according to his power that is at work within us*" (Ephesians 3:20).

Have you ever met someone who seems as if he or she has more of God working within than you do? I have! It can be intimidating. I have wondered how such people have so much of God's power and I don't. Is it a special gift from God? Or is it something that I can have also?

SEEK GOD

Ask Father to reveal to you His power in and for you. Ask Him how you can allow Him to work more mightily through you.

OBTAIN TRUTH

Commit this week's verse to memory.

Read Hebrews 11.

It's impossible to be a follower of Christ without faith. We have faith in God's Word and in Christ that He died for our sins. In Matthew 17:20, Jesus said to his disciples, "I tell you the truth, if you have faith as small as a mustard seed, you can say to this mountain, 'Move from here to there' and it will move. Nothing will be impossible for you."

God's power works through our faith.

Look at how Hebrews 11:1 defines faith: "Now faith is being sure of what we hope for and certain of what we do not see."

Now, this is very interesting: faith is being "*sure of what we hope for.*" Can you physically see what you hope for? No, first it has to be perceived. How do you perceive something that you do not see? You think and imagine it. You have to imagine it before you can hope for it.

You could say that your imagination ignites your hope. Faith happens after you have perceived something through your thoughts and imagination and then become certain of this thing that you cannot see.

God's power works through our faith. Now read about the people of faith in Hebrews 11. Write down all that you learn about their faith, dreams, and callings.

ABIDE

It is very likely that these "big faith" people were thankful to God. Why else would Noah agree to build an ark? Why would he commit 120 years of his life when it had never rained before? That makes no logical sense.

Noah had to have his mind and imagination laser-focused on God. His focus enabled him to hear, see, and carry out God's dreams for him.

Your imagination is always working. It is working for you (hope) or against you (despair)? In Romans 1:21, the thoughts and imaginations of men worked against them.

REACH OUT

Decide today: Will you surrender your imagination to God?

How do you surrender your imagination to God?

- Praise God at all times.
- Be thankful to God. Even if a situation seems unbearable, find something for which to be thankful
- Take captive any thoughts and imaginings that don't line up with the Bible:

- Casting down imaginations, and every high thing that exalteth itself against the knowledge of God, and bringing into captivity every thought to the obedience of Christ. (2 Corinthians 10:5 KJV)
- Read the Bible! Read Romans 10:17 to see how your faith can operate more effectively.

Day 3   Remember

Maybe your dreams have been suppressed because you have forgotten the wonderful works that God has done in the Word and in your own life.

SEEK GOD

Pray and meditate on this week's memory verse. Ask the Holy Spirit to give you wisdom and revelation to remember His hand in your life.

OBTAIN TRUTH

Review your memory verse today.

Read Psalm 8. Make two columns in your notebook, titled "God's Words and Actions" and "God's children's words and actions."

As you read along, write down your findings. When you are finished, answer these questions:

- On what do you think God's children were focused?
- What do you think His children were thinking and imagining?
- How did God respond?

ABIDE

Romans 1:21 says, "For although they knew God, they neither glorified him as God nor gave thanks to him, but their thinking became futile and their foolish hearts were darkened."

Notice this downward spiral of their thinking:

1. They did not glorify Him as God.

2. They didn't give thanks to Him.

3. Their thinking became futile.

4. Their hearts were darkened.

In Psalm 78:41, because God's children didn't remember the Lord's works, they vexed the Holy One of Israel. The Hebrew word translated as "vexed" can also be translated as "limited, pained, and provoked."

Matthew Henry's commentary suggests that the Israelites limited the Holy One to *their way* and *their timing*. They limited God because they didn't remember His great works and miracles. They didn't remember! They forgot how big, powerful, graceful, and mighty their God was because they were thinking about being hungry and not about being rescued.

Another way of limiting God is to tell Him how to fix your problems. I am guilty of this. I seem to think I know best and that God needs to get in line with my plan. For example, my husband owns a business. When we were in a very slow season, I prayed and asked God to give him enough work to feed our family.

Immediately after I said *"Amen,"* I remembered how much God loved my family and realized that it was nonsense to tell God how to care for us. I prayed, *"Father, scratch that. You love us. I know you will meet our needs. In this time, Father, just direct my husband's steps and show him how to use this free time. Show me how to love him in this season ... and how to be quiet."*

At first I prayed a limiting prayer. However, my replacement prayer fully trusted God with the outcome. He loves me and has my best interest at heart! I rest in that.

Have you limited God in your mind?

When we stop worshipping God and giving Him thanks, we can also limit God to our own way and timing. When our minds aren't remembering the awesome wonders He's done for us, worry, fear, panic, and despair set in.

God Himself cannot be limited. His purposes will be carried out. However, the extent to which you are used in those plans is up to your willingness to surrender your will to God's way.

REACH OUT

Before we can reach out, we need to remember the Lord's hand in our lives.

Today create a permanent record of God's goodness in your life. Record major battles that the Lord has won for you in the last five years. You can also write down some of the awesome miracles in the Bible—like when He parted the Red Sea!

Write down your list in a location where you can see it and read it daily. Our family places ours on sticky notes and writes them on our mirrors. Remember God's hand and goodness as the Spirit leads you.

This is one of my favorite things to do! It is an amazing thing to have when you are going through a battle. I whip out my list of victories and miracles to remind me of how good God has been. It strengthens me! Our God is for us! He wants us to remember that we can count on Him and He will make the desires of our heart His desires.

He wants all of your thoughts and imagination to be focused on His goodness and surrendered to Him. He wants to do more than you can ask, think, or imagine through you (Ephesians 3:20).

Now spend some time praising Him because He is for you!

Day 4   Rediscover

Yesterday we stirred up our minds and imaginations to remember how awesome our God is! Today you will create a "dream wall" by literally identifying and posting your dreams on a wall. Imagine the dream wall as a personal billboard, reminding you daily of your heart's desire.

This wall is an opportunity to stir up some old dreams that God planted in your heart. For me, my dreams were so suppressed that I was afraid to share them with anyone! Building the dream wall ripped off bandages that I had placed on my heart years before.

SEEK GOD

Spend some time in prayer. Ask God to show you His dreams for your life and to put His desires in your heart. Ask Him to direct your steps. Rest in God's presence and begin to ask Him for His desires for your life.

OBTAIN TRUTH

Read and review this week's memory verse.

Read Matthew 19:26, Mark 9:23, and Philippians 4:13.

What are some dreams you have that you think are impossible? How do these scriptures speak to those impossibilities?

Spend some time journaling about what these truths mean to you as you begin to rediscover how to dream.

ABIDE

Do you know what dreams you have that you want to fulfill? Do you know if those dreams are from God?

Jeremiah 29:11-13 tells us that the Lord has plans for each and every one of us. Yet how do we know what those plans are? How do we discern His will for our lives? The answer to that is found in Jeremiah 29:13: "You will seek me and find me, when you seek me with all your heart."

If you want to know God's plan for your life, spend time listening. He will open your eyes to the dreams and desires that He has for you.

When you humbly seek God, you can trust that He will direct your heart. In the Amplified version, Psalm 10:17 reads, "O Lord, You have heard the desire and the longing of the humble and oppressed; You will prepare and strengthen and direct their hearts, You will cause Your ear to hear."

REACH OUT

It's time to build your dream wall! Don't be intimidated. Some find it hard to let loose and dream. Remember, God will guide you. This is a simple way to trust God ... and not to worry about what anyone else—including you—thinks of your dreams!

The steps below are great fun with friends or family. Pull them together. Tell them that you need their help to uncover the dreams of your heart. Who can resist that request?

Here is what you need to do: *Share it! Stick it! Sort it! Step it! Share it!*

1. Grab some sticky notes, preferably the same color.

2. Ask yourself, "What would I like to see different in the world? If I could change something for the better, what would it be?" Dreams are often born out of the things that you love or the things that you can't stand.

3. Remember the unreasonable childhood dreams that you dismissed? Uncover your buried dreams. Dig out the dreams that others said were impossible.

4. Write every dream that you can think of on separate sticky notes. Keep them coming until you are drained of thoughts!

5. Post these sticky notes on the wall or somewhere easily viewed.

6. After you have exhausted brainstorming, you might find that some of your dreams are similar. Sort and group your sticky notes by similarity. Do you see a pattern of your passions?

7. Now for each group, sort your dreams from the simplest to the most difficult to accomplish. You want the dreams that are the most easily conquered at the top of the list.

8. You did it! In this simple step, God has revealed the passions in your heart. We will talk about next-steps tomorrow.

9. Celebrate the dreams that you have uncovered. Praise God!

Day 5   Taking Action

SEEK GOD

Rest in God's presence. Continue to seek God and ask Him to make His desires known.

OBTAIN TRUTH

Read Proverbs 3:5-6, Proverbs 16:9, and Matthew 6:25-34.

What are you responsible for? What has God promised you? Spend some time journaling about how these verses can motivate you as you dream.

ABIDE

How do you know if you are pursing the right dreams?

First, do not worry. If you are seeking after Jesus and renewing your mind, then you can trust that God's desires for you are in your heart.

Second, ask God to change your desires towards His dreams. Proverbs 16:9 says, "In his heart a man plans his course, but the Lord determines his steps." Ask God to direct your steps toward the dreams that He wants you to pursue and to curb your desires for the dreams that your flesh longs to accomplish.

Thirdly, remember simply to acknowledge Jesus in everything that you do (Proverbs 3:5-6). If you are acknowledging Jesus in everything, you can be certain that He will direct your steps.

Colossians 3:15 commands, "Let the peace of Christ rule in your hearts." If you don't have a deep internal peace about something, don't do it!

REACH OUT

It's time for the next step on your dream wall to turn your dreams into actions. This is simpler than you think!

Remember that earlier you sorted your dreams into similar categories. Then you decided which were easiest to accomplish.

Grab sticky notes—a different color from yesterday's. For each of these dreams, ask yourself this: "What is the next thing that I need to do in order to accomplish this dream?"

Think about the very simplest and next thing that needs to happen. For example, if your dream is to share Christ with the world, your very next step might be to meet your neighbors.

Write down only the very next step for each dream that is the easiest to accomplish. Then, before you do anything else ... take these steps! Don't start on any other dreams. Just do the next thing.

Why should you stay so focused on the next thing? Your spiritual enemy wants to distract and discourage you from God's dreams. Keep the enemy behind you with simple successes!

If you will be faithful in the smallest next thing, you will see God do a great work in your heart. Faithfulness in these small next-step actions will build your hope and faith to do the next thing after that. Remember, an object in motion wants to stay in motion!

After you have completed the next step, you can take the second, third, and fourth steps, and so on ... one at a time. Before you know it, you have accomplished a dream!

This process helped me train my mind and physical body, my temple, to submit to the Spirit of God rather than to my natural impulses.

Now is a great time to share your dream wall with someone you love and trust. Don't be afraid to invite others into your dreams. Those who love you most can support you, pray for you, encourage you, and help you do more than you could ever do on your own!

CRAVE

Write down a list of people with whom to share your dream wall this week.

Many are suffering from dream suppression. Revive someone's dreams today!

REACH OUT– Week Five
Multiply with Teamwork (with Sheri and Amy)

Memory Verse:

> "The harvest is plentiful, but the workers are few. Ask the Lord of the harvest, therefore, to send out workers into his harvest field." (Luke 10:2)

Video Review: http://www.soarwithgod.com/Reach/Reach.html

Are you a "do it all, be it all" person?

Jesus believed in teams!

> After this the Lord appointed seventy-two others and sent them two by two (36 groups) ahead of him to every town and place where he was about to go. He told them, "The harvest is plentiful, but the workers are few. Ask the Lord of the harvest, therefore, to send out workers into his *harvest field*. (Luke 10:1-2)

To grow and multiply, teamwork is a must!

Benefits of Teamwork

- Friendship
- Efficiency
- Shared Load
- Effectiveness
- Glorifies God

Say "yes" to community and relationships!

Day 1   A Multiplying Mission Field

SEEK GOD

Pray for the Kingdom of God to multiply! Ask the Father to continue to send out teams of believers into the entire world to share the Gospel.

OBTAIN TRUTH

Meditate on and review this week's memory verse. Take the time to commit it to memory in order to help renew your mind.

Read Acts 1:8. As you read this verse, write down the order of ministry. Where should ministry begin? Notice the outward progression. Have you ever missed any of these steps along the way?

ABIDE

Have you ever thrown a rock into water? What do you see? Ripples. Ripples start at the point of impact and continue out from that point.

Jesus faithfully empowered and called His disciples to be witnesses. Jesus began the Great Ripple that would eventually reach the likes of you and me some two-thousand years later!

A similar effect can be true for us. What if an outreach effort began with you?

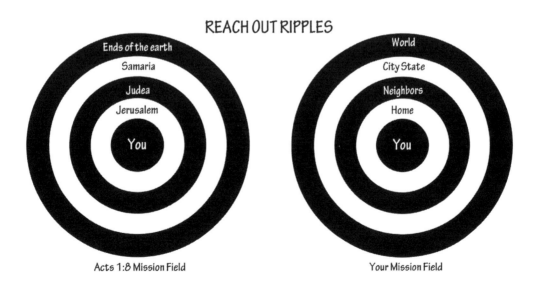

REACH OUT RIPPLES

Acts 1:8 Mission Field

Your Mission Field

When you throw a rock into water, you cannot stop it from making ripples; it is just a natural process. This should happen to you as well. As the power and love of God transform you, you'll naturally flow into others in His love.

Once your heart is in love with God, reaching out is a supernatural response, not a dutiful work. It just becomes who you are.

Imagine the mighty ripples that can take place when God's uses *you* to reach out—and the effect that this will have in your circle of influence, all for God's glory. As God multiplies, that ripple will continue to impact future generations!

Often, reaching out starts with those closest to you and eventually works its way outward. But it takes time and God's power to multiply!

Reach out right where you are. Start at home. I have seen too many people minister to others while their home life was on the verge of breaking apart.

You cannot effectively minister until you lose your life. It is in losing your life that you find it (Read Matthew 16:25).

Jesus proclaimed in John 12:24, "I tell you the truth, unless a kernel of wheat falls to the ground and dies, it remains only a single seed. But if it dies, it produces many seeds."

REACH OUT

Pray and ask Father God to reveal where He wants to multiply through you. Where should you reach out—in your home, work, neighborhood, city, or state, or in a foreign country? God is faithful. He will direct you.

Worship God for the loving Ripple of Jesus Christ that is washing over you!

Evaluate your mission fields:

My Heart

Has God invaded my life and radically changed me? Do I seek God daily in prayer and in His Word? If you are reading this, then most likely, you are seeking God. When this study ends, will your pursuit continue?

Home

How's my home life? Am I respectful and honoring of others in my home (my spouse, children, siblings, or parents)? Do I serve lovingly, without selfish motives? If you said "no" to any of these questions, it's time to start being a minister in your home.

Neighbors

Do your neighbors love and follow Christ? If not, write their names down on a list and pray for them. Ask God to reveal ways to minister to them. Maybe you need to start by meeting your neighbors!

To me, neighbors are also the people with whom we share our daily life— co-workers, a housekeeper, the dry-cleaners, the grocer, extended family, friends, school buddies, teammates, the local treatment center, and so on. Are you serving and sharing the love of Christ with your neighbors? Write down a few ways to demonstrate love to them.

City or State

Do you know the needs and opportunities in your city? If you haven't already researched this, maybe it's time to get started.

What is the teen pregnancy rate? Is there a prison ministry in your area? How many foster kids or homeless people are there in your state? Are there ministries that feed and provide for local impoverished families—and do they need volunteers or other assistance?

You will not know how to serve if you don't know the needs and the opportunities in your own state.

World

Some people are called to go to a foreign nation to raise up Christ-followers. Is this you?

Whether you're called to live abroad or not, there are many ways to have a global impact right from your home.

Two ways to help you start today:

- *Pray!* There are many resources that can help direct you in what and how to pray. One of my favorites is the VOM Prayer Calendar, which is now available as a phone application for iPhone and Android.
- *Give!* You can give money to help dig water wells, provide disaster relief, fight human trafficking, sponsor a child, or support a missionary. You don't have to be wealthy to make a difference. Your generosity will make Kingdom ripples no matter the amount!

If you believe you are called to minister abroad, seek God. Trust Him to guide your path. Many wonderful international ministries exist, yet many are still to be birthed. Ask God to show you if you are to partner with a ministry or begin a new work. Write out additional, specific prayers and action steps to take.

Day 2   Multiply on the Home Front

SEEK GOD

Pray for salvation and love to multiply in your home.

OBTAIN TRUTH

How do you memorize best? Find a method to help you remember this week's verse.

Read Mark 5:1-20 and write down your findings:

- When the restored man asked Jesus if he could go join Him and the disciples, what was Jesus' response? Where did the man's ministry start as a result?
- What obstacles could have stopped this man from sharing his story with others?

ABIDE

What fear or limitation is holding you back from reaching out right where you are—fear, embarrassment, pride, or lack of knowledge?

Consider what impact the restored man would have had if he had given in to such thoughts as these:

- What difference can I make? My family will never listen to me.
- I don't have time to share my story—I have too much ministry work to do.
- I don't know any Bible verses. I'm just a baby Christian, and someone else would do a better job telling them about Christ.
- What if they reject me or don't believe me?

What excuses have kept you from sharing your faith in your home and community?

Your role is to reach out faithfully. God's role is to multiply faithfully.

REACH OUT

Everyone has a story. What is your story? How did Jesus change your life?

If asked, could you share your story in sixty seconds? Five minutes? Ask God to help you narrow in on your story. Write it down. Practice your story so you will be ready to share it.

Read Galatians 1. Notice how Paul shared his testimony and the Gospel.

Write the heading "Paul's convictions and concerns about the task of sharing the Gospel" in your notebook. Record all of your discoveries.

I love how Paul shared his testimony in two short verses in Galatians 1:13-14. In verse 15, however, he basically said, "…but God!" Then Paul spent the rest of Galatians talking about God's grace. In this example, God gets the glory, not Paul's awful, sin-filled past. He spent more time declaring God's redemptive work than on his many past failures.

Keep your eyes open this week for opportunities to share your story!

Day 3   Multiply Together

I (Amy) really like eating a great dinner followed by watching a classic movie for a little rest and relaxation. Entertainment and eating are some of the most pleasurable things we do in life. But not if we are alone! To me, there's something significantly missing when life's joys, sorrows, and even the mundane are experienced in solitude.

We aren't meant to live in seclusion. You and I were God-ordained for teamwork, celebrations, marriage, families, communities, and cooperation. Together we build, laugh, dance, learn, work, love, mourn, inspire, encourage, worship, pray, battle—I could go on and on.

Today we are going to look at the significance of our relationships with people.

SEEK GOD

Praise and give thanks to God for your relationships.

OBTAIN TRUTH

Review your memory verse by reading it aloud twice.

Read Matthew 4:18-22 and John 1:35-51.

What was Jesus is doing in these passages? And more importantly, why?

ABIDE

Jesus recruited a group of men to be by His side at the onset of His public ministry. These disciples became students or mentees under Jesus' tutelage because Jesus was after multiplication. Jesus knew that to transfer the Kingdom's Gospel message effectively to the ends of the earth, He would need transformed and trained followers.

Scripture reveals that Jesus' disciples became his friends and met many of His practical support and fellowship needs. One example of this is at the Garden of Gethsemane in Mark 14:34, when Jesus said, "My soul is overwhelmed with sorrow to the point of death..." He said to them. "Stay here and keep watch."

If Jesus needed others in His life, how much more do we? You can do some good on your own, but being part of a team will bring a far greater impact! Increase the Kingdom's influence by working alongside others for a common goal. Multiply!

> Two are better than one, because they have a good return for their work: If one falls down, his friend can help him up. But pity the man who falls and has no one to help him up! Also, if two lie down together, they will keep warm. But how can one keep warm alone? Though one may be overpowered, two can defend themselves. A cord of three strands is not quickly broken. (Ecclesiastes 4:9-12)

REACH OUT

- Who are you doing life with?
- Are you serving alongside other believers as a team?
- Who's on your life's board of directors? These people are significant and direct voices in your life. Have you told them that they sit on your board?
- Are you in a consistent small-group with other believers?
- Do you have a friend who holds you accountable?
- Is there someone committed to pray for and with you?
- Do you have a mentor/mentee relationship with someone?
- Are you intentionally engaged and encouraging with those living in your home?

If you need more community, ask God to lead you to the right relationships. He will show you if there's a person or group with whom you need to connect.

Day 4   Teamwork

SEEK GOD

Focus your heart, mind, and strength on prayer with your Father. Ask Him to reveal an area of your life in which you need to ask for and receive assistance.

OBTAIN TRUTH

Review your memory verse.

Read Exodus 18:13-27.

Write "What a Thriving Ministry Needs" as your notebook's next title page. Record your observations. Be sure to process the text for less-obvious insights too.

Consider Moses' decision to accept Jethro's plan:

- Why do you think Moses did all of this work by himself?
- What do you suppose Moses had to sacrifice to allow others to lead with him?
- What do you think he gained from this change?
- What did the people gain?

ABIDE

Have you ever thought, "If it's going to be, then it's up to me" and then set out to accomplish a goal alone? If so, what do you think led you to this attitude and decision?

Consider the following possibilities:

- The last time someone helped, it proved to be more trouble than it was worth.
- You didn't know whom to ask.
- You were too impatient and busy to stop and ask for help.
- You were sure no one else could do the task as well as you.
- Other: _____

Identify one or two of the situations above that you've experienced. Is there a root cause, going deeper than these statements, that you need to deal with? Let God do a work in you right now. Don't wait until you're overwhelmed with too much on your plate before trying to figure out a better plan.

Like Moses, I (Amy) have tried to do it all and be all to everyone. It took years for me to learn to say the word "no." I'm still learning the art of delegating and building up a team of leaders. These lessons are vital for healthy, sustainable ministry, and I'm committed to mastering them.

Are you growing as a leader? Are you willing to do so?

REACH OUT

Spend time in thoughtful prayer.

Is there someone you need to join, or ask to join you, in a certain task?

Ask God to show you where you need to make changes in your ministry. By the way, all of a Christian's life is ministry. You are an ambassador called to live as Christ!

Day 5   Sowing and Reaping

> As long as the earth endures, seedtime and harvest, cold and heat, summer and winter, day and night will never cease. (Genesis 8:22)

SEEK GOD

Spend time with your Father today. Ask Him to make you usable for His purposes, not your own. He will!

OBTAIN TRUTH

Review today's memory verse.

Read Matthew 13:1-43. How does God naturally multiply on this earth? What obstacles prevent it?

ABIDE

God created the world with a seedtime and a harvest time.

The reproducing process for which God provided in nature, He expects also from His children in supernatural fruit. The good fruit that we grow and bear in our lives is multiplied through small seeds—seeds that were at one time sown in us.

A good seed of faith is sown through reading, hearing, and applying the truth of the Word of God. Other believers may have sown seeds of faith and love in your spirit as well.

Sown seeds are designed to reproduce; but seeds that are unused remain unchanged. There can be no new life without seed sowing.

Write down the names of the people who have sown good seed into your life. What did they do?

_____

_____

_____

Now multiply their work! Imitate them and sow new seeds into others' lives from your personal harvest.

What are you currently sowing? What will it reap? Pray and ask God for insight into this. Each person will have a different response. The Lord is speaking to you. Are you listening for His whispers?

> Do not be deceived: God cannot be mocked. A man reaps what he sows. The one who sows to please his sinful nature, from that nature will reap destruction; the one who sows to please the Spirit, from the Spirit will reap eternal life. Let us not become weary in doing good, for at the proper time we will reap a harvest if we do not give up. Therefore, as we have opportunity, let us do good to all people, especially to those who belong to the family of believers. (Galatians 6:7-10)

REACH OUT

> "Anyone can count the seeds in an apple, but only God can count the number of apples in a seed." ~ Robert H. Schuller

God is the multiplier of all that you plant and harvest. He knows the outcome, so you don't have to worry about the results. When you stop to count your results, you aren't working. Stop counting and measuring; just sow and reap.

Ask God where you should be sowing.

> Remember this: Whoever sows sparingly will also reap sparingly, and whoever sows generously will also reap generously ... Now he who supplies seed to the sower and bread for food will also supply and increase your store of seed and will enlarge the harvest of your righteousness. (2 Corinthians 9:6 and 10)

Next week we are going to talk more about sowing and reaping.

CRAVE

When you reach out together, there will be opportunities for strife or unity. Decide to be a peacemaker. Check out what Jesus says about unity below:

> "I have given them the glory that you gave me, that they may be one as we are one—I in them and you in me. May they be brought to complete unity to let the world know that you sent me and have loved them even as you have loved me." (John 17:22-23)

This unity among God's children is what Jesus said would cause the world to know that Jesus is the Son of God.

Read the following verses. Write down "Unity is..." as a title in your notebook and fill in your insights from these scriptures:

Psalm 133:1;

John 17:20-23;

Romans 6:5;

Colossians 3:14;

1 Corinthians 1, 2, and 3;

Ephesians 4

REACH OUT – Week Six
Good News (with Amy and Sheri)

Memory Verse:

> Go into all the world and preach the Good News to everyone. (Mark 16:15 NLT)

What is the Good News? When I (Sheri) was a child, my church urged us to accept Jesus so that we wouldn't go to hell. When I heard about this place of fire, I took the insurance policy. Hey, I'm not stupid! But I thought that salvation was only a destination. The Good News is so much more than that!

This week, we are going to define the "Good News," including what it means to you and how to share it in your daily life. At the end of this week's study, you will be strengthened and ready to reach out.

Video Review: http://www.soarwithgod.com/Reach/Reach.html

Share the good news with urgency and boldness.

Are you actively sharing Christ?

Roadblocks to Sharing Christ:

- Fear
- Uncertainty how
- Making assumptions
- Living in Christian bubble
- Busyness

An *urgent* attitude comes from understanding the severity of the consequences: *Hell*.

Prepare to share Christ.

> But in your hearts set apart Christ as Lord. Always be prepared to give an answer to everyone who asks you to give the reason for the hope that you have. But do this with gentleness and respect. (1 Peter 3:15)

Urgency results in *boldness*.

Be bold! Paul requested, "And pray for me, too. Ask God to give me the right words so I can boldly explain God's mysterious plan that the Good News is for Jews and Gentiles alike" (Ephesians 6:19 NLT).

God draws man to himself.

> No one can come to me unless the Father who sent me draws him, and I will raise him up at the last day. (John 6:44)

> ...I make myself a slave to everyone, to win as many as possible. To the Jews I became like a Jew, to win the Jews ... To the weak I became weak, to win the weak. I have become all things to all men so that by all possible means I might save some. I do all this for the sake of the gospel, that I may share in its blessings. (1 Corinthians 9:19-20, 22)

Who would you regret not sharing Christ with certain other people in your life if they were to die today?

Day 1   Not-So-Good News

To understand the Good News, it's important to understand the not-so-good news—Hell. Hell is real.

SEEK GOD

Ask Jesus to give you understanding today. Try praying this prayer:

Father, grant me revelation from your Word. Ignite in me a passion to tell others about you. Interrupt me. Awaken me. Lord, place in my path unbelievers so I can share Your life and love. In Jesus' name, amen.

OBTAIN TRUTH

Read Luke 16:19-31 and Matthew 25:31-46.

Title a new page "Hell is..." Make an exhaustive list of your findings. Use your imagination to enhance your understanding.

Now answer the following questions:

- Is the rich man in Hell because of the way he treated Lazarus?
- Is the rich man ever able to escape his torment?
- Why is Lazarus not able to go to the rich man?
- Would Lazarus or someone else want to go help the rich man?

ABIDE

Have you ever flown in first class? I haven't. On an eight-hour flight home from Hawaii, the business-class passengers in front of us laid their chairs back (they were now in our faces). I slept off and on, but my poor husband did not sleep one minute. He was miserable. He constantly looked longingly through the dividing wall at the first-class seats, feeling envious and pondering why he hadn't spent the extra money for better seats.

It reminded me of this story in Luke. The rich man could see the comfort and blessed life that Christ's children enjoyed while he suffered.

Hell is real. I have heard many people say, "How could a good God make good people suffer in such an awful place?"

Hell's original purpose was not for man, but for the devil and his angels:

> "Then he will say to those on his left, 'Depart from me, you who are cursed, into the eternal fire prepared for the devil and his angels." (Matthew 25:41)

God doesn't want man in Hell. He doesn't want any man to perish, but to have eternal life.

> The Lord is not slow in keeping his promise, as some understand slowness. He is patient with you, *not wanting anyone to perish, but everyone to come to repentance*. (2 Peter 3:9 *emphasis added*)

As you read the text in Matthew, however, you see that sin caused a huge problem, which those who do not know the Lord must face. Yet glorious Good News is coming on Day 2. Read on. Stay with us!

REACH OUT

After completing today's homework, is there really anyone who you dislike enough that you would want him or her to spend eternity in hell like the rich man? What about the people you love? No, of course not. You would not even want them to suffer here on earth.

The problem is that we do not like to think about the consequences of not knowing and believing in Jesus. If we refrain from sharing Christ, in essence we are leaving them to a certain fate. That's not okay with me.

You have an awesome opportunity to share the greatest gift with your family, your neighbors, and the world! Do not see it as a burden, an embarrassment, or a non-urgent matter. It is urgent. Jesus calls us to do this: "Go into all the world and preach the good news to all creation" (Mark 16:15 NLT).

God wants you to spread the Word. He wants you to tell others about what He has done for you. He wants everyone to hear His Good News. He doesn't want even one person denied the opportunity to be saved.

Write down the names of people you know who do not personally know and believe in Jesus. Pray for them. Begin to reach out to them.

However, refuse to stop there. Do not be afraid to spread the name of Jesus to every person you know and meet. Maybe it's your server at a restaurant. Maybe it's the clerk you see every time you go to a gas station. Maybe it's someone you see regularly at the gym.

Ask the Holy Spirit to guide you as you seek to tell others about Jesus.

Day 2   Good News

SEEK GOD

Thank you, Father, for becoming a man so that you could save me! Father, equip me to share your sacrifice with every person in my path. I ask for words of knowledge and insight to speak Your truth into others. I want to share Your love.

Father, make me bold. Help me to become a selfless laborer. Make me usable. I surrender and give You freedom to do with my life whatever Your heart desires. I am all in. May Your way be my way, Father! In Jesus' name, amen.

OBTAIN TRUTH

To share life with others, you must deeply understand your own need for a Savior. You must fully understand that Jesus suffered for you. You must dig deep. Don't grow weary. Allow God to do His work in and through you!

Review this week's memory verse.

Read John 19 and Isaiah 52:13-53:12.

Label a new page "The Good News is..." and "How Jesus suffered for me." Reread the text, but this time think about, and write down, "Why Jesus suffered for me."

ABIDE

Reviewing the message of God's Good News will help us be sharp and ready to share it at any moment. Take a fresh look at some key scriptures that are useful when communicating the Gospel:

> For all have sinned and fall short of the glory of God. (Romans 3:23)

Every person falls short of God's righteousness and needs a Savior. One sin equals death. It's that simple. It's not how far you fall short. It's that you *do* fall short.

> For whoever keeps the whole law and yet stumbles at just one point is guilty of breaking all of it. (James 2:10)

Some might argue, "Well, I am not as bad as Hitler, so how could God send me to hell? Isn't He a loving God? Surely a loving God wouldn't do that!"

God does not take sin lightly: "*For the wages of sin is death...*" (Romans 6:23a).

Some cannot understand the offensiveness of sin. God will not just change His mind about sin. Sin must be judged.

Jesus was God manifested in human body. His life was worth more than all our lives together. He was holy and pure. Jesus took the punishment for the sins of the whole world. God put all our sins onto Jesus, whose blood paid for every individual sin, including lying, murder, stealing, greed, homosexuality, and so on.

> He is the atoning sacrifice for our sins, and not only for ours but also for the sins of the whole world. (1 John 2:2)

Get ready. Are you paying attention? If you can understand this then you can understand why there is a hell:

> When he (talking about the Holy Spirit) comes, he will convict the world of guilt in regard to sin and righteousness and judgment: in regard to sin, *because men do not believe in me*. (John 16:8-9)

The only sin outstanding against mankind is rejecting Jesus. Thereby you reject the awesome price that He paid for you to be free. You neglect the opportunity to know God and to have eternal life. The wages of sin is death, but Jesus took your place! God did not recall His word or this consequence. He paid it for you!

Hell is for those who reject God Almighty. He loved them enough to come to earth as a man and die for their sins. Sin caused a huge problem, but God Himself paid the full price!

This is the Good News! This is the Gospel that Jesus talks about in this week's memory verse.

REACH OUT

Now that you've reviewed the Good News, could you put it in your own words to be prepared to share? Consider writing it down, vocally recording it, or meditating on it.

Practice in your small group or with family, friends, or a co-worker.

Day 3   No Plan B

SEEK GOD

Give God thanks today. Thank Him for opening the eyes of your heart. Thank Him for saving you and for all that He has done for you!

OBTAIN TRUTH

Review this week's memory verse.

Read Mark 16:14-20 and Acts 2:14-41.

Whom did Jesus commission in Mark? What did He commission them to do?

ABIDE

Jesus didn't have a "Plan B." He left His entire ministry with the eleven men He had trained for three years. We are followers of Christ today because these men faithfully shared the Good News with someone.

God doesn't have a Plan B today, either. He is counting on you and me to share His message—the Good News!

REACH OUT

You are called, commanded, and commissioned! What are you going to do about it? Write down something short-term and something long-term and add these to your dream wall. Do not delay!

Day 4   One Matters

SEEK GOD

Ask God to provide opportunities for you to express your faith with lost people. Ask Him to multiply one person into thousands.

OBTAIN TRUTH

Review this week's memory verse.

Read Matthew 18:12-14.

Write down answers to the following questions:

- Why was one sheep so important when there were still 99 left?
- Why do you think God is so willing to go after the one that is lost?
- Do you think God calls us to do the same? Why?
- What are some ways in which you think God reaches out to His "lost sheep"?
- How can you begin reaching out to the "lost sheep," practically?
- How can you realistically bring in a harvest of one hundred? One thousand? One million or one billion?

ABIDE

Have you stopped trying to reach out to someone because you think it is a waste of time? Have you grown weary in sharing the name of Jesus?

> Let us not become weary in doing good, for at the proper time we will reap a harvest if we do not give up. (Galatians 6:9)

We cannot grow weary! We may never know how much of an impact we have on someone. God's Word does not return void.

> "So is my word that goes out from my mouth: It will not return to me empty, but will accomplish what I desire and achieve the purpose for which I sent it."
> (Isaiah 55:11)

Trust and listen to the Holy Spirit to lead you where you need to be.

REACH OUT

Start by reaching out to one person. Teach him or her to be a disciple of Jesus. When that person is ready, send him or her out. Let this person become the teacher. God will multiply from one life committed to Him.

Consider investing in a group of people. You could work together to learn how to train others to be disciples of Jesus. Even having just three other people in your group can start a chain reaction.

Billy Graham preached the Gospel in person to more people than anyone else in history. According to his staff, more than 3.2 million people responded to accept the Savior, Jesus Christ, at Billy Graham Crusades.

His own personal relationship with Christ can be traced back to a Sunday school teacher. Look at this chain of conversions:

- Sunday School teacher Edward Kimball helped lead Dwight L. Moody to Christ;
- J. Wilbur Chapman was converted at a Dwight L. Moody evangelistic meeting;
- Billy Sunday was converted at a Chapman meeting;
- Mordecai Ham was converted at Billy Sunday meeting;
- Billy Graham was converted at a Ham meeting.

One person can make a BIG difference!

You can read more about Graham's conversion in the second chapter of his autobiography, *Just As I Am* (HarperCollins, 1997).

Day 5   Grace is for the Humbled

SEEK GOD

Spend a quiet moment with the Father. Ask Him to open up opportunities for you to share His good news of salvation.

OBTAIN TRUTH

Practice your memory verse today.

Read Luke 18:9-27 and Luke 19:1-10.

Write the titles "The Self-Righteous" and "The Humble" in your notebook. Record the characteristics you see in these two kinds of people. Also answer these questions:

- In what ways did Jesus reach out to these men?
- What were the rich man's problems?
- What does wealth possess that causes man to stumble?
- Why do you suppose that Zacchaeus was ripe for salvation?

ABIDE

I (Amy) was a child when I asked Jesus to forgive and save me. I still remember realizing the gravity of my sin and my need for a Savior. That night, at an outdoor revival, I came to Jesus as a humble desperate child, and my life forever changed.

From the way that Jesus lived and walked on the earth, we see that He wanted everyone to repent and be saved. He could supernaturally discern men's hearts and know who was ripe for the harvest.

The *self-righteous* and proud do not see that they are lost. Or they simply aren't willing to lay down the things of the world for the One True Thing. We need to pray for the lost, proud person to be humbled—to have darkened eyes opened to his or her need for the Savior.

Do you know anyone who is self-righteous and lost?

Humbled people know that they are in need. We need to be ready to recognize the broken people around us who are ripening for a harvest. This could likely include a person who has been going through a significant trial. Suffering may have brought him or her to a place of humility and searching for spiritual truth.

Some people are also ripe to receive Christ at the top of their game (this was my husband, Craig). Life's pleasures and successes have proven empty and meaningless, and they're desperate for lasting peace.

Do you know someone in one of these situations? Pray for an opportunity to share Christ with this person!

REACH OUT

Stop. Take a moment and think about what life was like when you were lost. Remember all that changed for you after you repented and were forgiven.

Make a commitment to seek actively to share the Good News with someone who is in humble or proud circumstances.

Write down the names of at least two people for whom you can pray and with whom you can share Christ.

This week, declare God's plan for salvation with someone on your list. If you discover that this person already knows Christ, then rejoice! But if the person does not know Him, how can you keep silent?

Love others enough to overcome any fear or discomfort. God's love was poured out for them as well as for you. Reach out to someone today!

CRAVE

Read Revelation 8, 9 and 10.

Write down a journal heading, "End Times." When my eight-year-old read these chapters, she immediately gained an urgency to share the Gospel with everyone! She shares with others and asks us to, even when we are reluctant.

Even though no one knows when the end times will happen (Mark 13:32), these are *your* end times. Your life is short. James 4:14 says, "What is your life? You are a mist that appears for a little while and then vanishes." Make your life count!

We added this commentary to this week's study because it gives insight into the suffering of Jesus Christ. Rejecting this amazing gift is the greatest sin of all! Reach out to someone today.

Just consider the deep agony that Jesus faced for you and for all people in this world. We pray that this gives you a broken heart for the lost and suffering.

Matthew Henry's Commentary on Luke 22:41-44 explains:

> That, when Christ was in his agony, there appeared to him an angel from heaven, strengthening him, v. 43. (1.) It was an instance of the deep humiliation of our Lord Jesus that he needed the assistance of an angel, and would admit it. The influence of the divine nature withdrew for the present, and then, as to his human nature, he was for a little while lower than the angels, and was capable of receiving help from them. (2.) When he was not delivered from his sufferings, yet he was strengthened and supported under them, and that was equivalent. If God proportion the shoulders

to the burden, we shall have no reason to complain, whatever he is pleased to lay upon us. David owns this a sufficient answer to his prayer, in the day of trouble, that God strengthened him with strength in his soul, and so does the son of David, Psalm 138:3. (3.) The angels ministered to the Lord Jesus in his sufferings. He could have had legions of them to rescue him; nay, this one could have done it, could have chased and conquered the whole band of men that came to take him; but he made use of his ministration only to strengthen him; and the very visit which this angel made him now in his grief, when his enemies were awake and his friends asleep, was such a seasonable token of the divine favor as would be a very great strengthening to him. Yet this was not all: he probably said something to him to strengthen him; put him in mind that his sufferings were in order to his Father's glory, to his own glory, and to the salvation of those that were given him, represented to him the joy set before him, the seed he should see; with these and the like suggestions he encouraged him to go on cheerfully; and what is comforting is strengthening. Perhaps he did something to strengthen him, wiped away his sweat and tears, perhaps ministered some cordial to him, as after his temptation, or, it may be, took him by the arm, and helped him off the ground, or bore him up when he was ready to faint away; and in these services of the angel the Holy Spirit was putting strength into him; for so the word signifies. It pleased the Lord to bruise him indeed; yet did he plead against him with his great power? No, but he put strength in him (Job 23:6), as he had promised, Psalm 89:21; Isaiah. 49:8; 50:7.

2. That, being in an agony, he prayed more earnestly, v. 44. As his sorrow and trouble grew upon him, he grew more importunate in prayer; not that there was before any coldness or indifference in his prayers, but there was now a greater vehemency in them, which was expressed in his voice and gesture. Note, Prayer, though never out of season, is in a special manner seasonable when we are in an agony; and the stronger our agonies are the more lively and frequent our prayers should be. Now it was that Christ offered up prayers and supplications with strong crying and tears, and was heard in that he feared (Hebrews 5:7), and in his fear wrestled, as Jacob with the angel.

3. That, in this agony, his sweat was as it were great drops of blood falling down to the ground. Sweat came in with sin, and was a branch of the curse, Genesis 3:19. And therefore, when Christ was made sin and a curse for us, he underwent a grievous sweat, that in the sweat of his face we might eat bread, and that he might sanctify and sweeten all our trials to us. There is some dispute among the critics whether this sweat is only compared to drops of blood, being much thicker than drops of sweat commonly are, the pores of the body being more than ordinarily

opened, or whether real blood out of the capillary veins mingled with it, so that it was in color like blood, and might truly be called a bloody sweat; the matter is not great. Some reckon this one of the times when Christ shed his blood for us, for without the shedding of blood there is no remission. Every pore was as it were a bleeding wound, and his blood stained all his raiment. This showed the travail of his soul. He was now abroad in the open air, in a cool season, upon the cold ground, far in the night, which, one would think, had been enough to strike in a sweat; yet now he breaks out into a sweat, which bespeaks the extremity of the agony he was in.

Congratulations!
You have completed the SOAR Bible study.

If you are still hungry to know more, open up your Bible and try some of our "After the Study" work on the following pages.

Our prayer for you has been that you would fall more in love with God and obtain your own revelation of who God is and who you are—and then go into the world to share it!

Send us your feedback on Facebook.

Love,

Amy and Sheri

SOAR Bible Study

www.soarwithgod.com

Our Church Home

www.Lifechurch.tv – Worship online from anywhere!

Amy Groeschel   www.amygroeschel.com

Sheri Yates   www.ikanministries.com

AFTER THE STUDY: OBTAIN

Your journey in obtaining truth doesn't have to stop here. Our prayer is that you will desire to continue studying God's Word on your own or with a small group in order to obtain even more revelation of God's truth. The Scripture is active and alive. If you choose to seek it, it will meet you where you are and bring life to your circumstances. There are infinite revelations to be found in the Word. It is a treasure waiting to be sought out!

Instead of starting a different Bible study, try grabbing a new journal and reading the Word as if you were on a treasure hunt. Search for things like "Who is God?" or reuse some of the journal headings from this study.

Consider taking a tour through the epistles. They are the letters written to the early church. In much of the material here, you can clearly see God's grace, love, and mercy as well as who you are in Christ. Pick one of the epistles listed below. Then title a journal page with one of the headings listed to the right.

1 Corinthians	2 Corinthians	Galatians
Ephesians	Philippians	Colossians
1 Thessalonians	2 Thessalonians	1 Timothy
2 Timothy	Titus	Philemon

Take one book or one chapter at a time—it's up to you. This process is going to help you get the truth from the source of truth, God Himself. Your view of God will be strengthened as you get outside of your comfort zone to seek God and obtain truth by faith!

Journal Page Headings

Listed below are ideas for journal topics that might be beneficial in your pursuit of revelation. Use these suggestions or make up your own!

- "God's Character" or "Attributes of God"
- "Who is God?"
- "Who Does God Say I Am?"
- "God's Role"
- "My Role"
- "Product of Sin"
- "Product of Walking by the Spirit"
- "My Calling"
- "Why Obey God?"
- "Blessings"
- "God Loves Me"
- "What Belongs to Me"
- "Instructions to Believers"
- "Warnings to Believers"
- "Adoption Manual"

AFTER THE STUDY: ABIDE

Your journey in obtaining truth doesn't have to stop here. Our prayer is that you will desire to continue studying God's Word on your own or with a small group in order to attain even more revelation of God's truth. The Scripture is active and alive. If you choose to seek it, it will meet you where you are and bring life to your circumstances. There are infinite revelations to be found in the Word. It is a treasure waiting to be sought out!

Instead of starting a different Bible study, try grabbing a new journal and reading the Word as if you were on a treasure hunt.

Consider taking a tour through the gospel books. Read through Matthew, Mark, Luke, and John. These are referred to as the four gospels. They depict the life and ministry of Christ.

Consider the following journal headings:

- "Lessons from a Miracle of Jesus"
- "How Did Jesus Abide?"
- "Jesus' Love"
- "The Kingdom of God"
- "Lessons from the Life of..."
- "Faith"
- "My Authority"
- "My Hope"
- "What did Jesus Do?"
- "My Calling"

Try making up your own journal page headings. This is what we do:

As we see a consistent theme, we write it at the top of our page. Then we write down all of the truths in that theme. Enjoy this eye-opening study method!

Acknowledgments

SOAR took us approximately four years to write and record while we were carrying on with our daily family responsibilities.

It was a wonderful journey of deepening sisterhood, friendship and transformation for many that joined us along the journey.

All praise and glory to our Savior, Jesus Christ. Without His overwhelming love, we wouldn't know how to share His Truth with others through SOAR.

Thank you so much to Lifechurch.tv for all your support, effort, videoing, editing and mostly for believing in us!

Thank you especially to Kevin Ely and the entire Lifechurch.tv Bling team. Kevin, you personally were bold in your feedback and encouragement. Because of that we improved over time!

Smith Pixels, thank you for wrapping up the video edits with excellence.

Rawchurch.tv, thank you for believing in us and helping us fund this project.

Addition To our children: Catie, Mandy, Anna, Sam, Stephen, Joy, Spencer, Chandler, and Kennedi, we are so thankful for your loving and patient support as we worked on SOAR. We love you to infinity and beyond!

Thank you to our husbands for ordering take-out and picking up kids while we were busy. Craig and Ty, you were a constant source of encouragement and support!

To all the volunteers, small group leaders, and teams that helped us record and edit SOAR, thank you with all our hearts.

9995561R00145